Aristophanes

Clouds

Aristophanes

Clouds

Translated, with Notes, by Peter Meineck

Introduction by Ian C. Storey

Hackett Publishing Company, Inc.
Indianapolis/Cambridge

For further information, please address:
  Hackett Publishing Company, Inc.
  PO Box 44937
  Indianapolis, IN 46244-0937

  www.hackettpublishing.com

          Library of Congress Cataloging-in-Publication Data

Aristophanes.
     [Clouds. English]
     Clouds / Aristophanes ; translated, with notes, by Peter Meineck :
introduction by Ian C. Storey.
        p. cm.
     ISBN 0-87220-517-7 — ISBN 0-87220-516-9 (pbk.)
     I. Meineck, Peter, 1967–   II. Title.
   PA3877.N8   2000
   882'.01—dc21   99-058753

ISBN-13: 978-0-87220-517-8 (cloth)
ISBN-13: 978-0-87220-516-1 (pbk.)

The paper used in this publication meets the minimum requirements of
American National Standard for Information Sciences—Permanence of
Paper for Printed Library Materials, ANSI Z39.48–1984.
                                   ∞

Contents

Introduction   vii

Diagram of the Stage   xlii

Translator's Preface   xliii

Cast of Characters   2

Clouds   3

Endnotes   101

Appendix: The First Version of *Clouds*   115

Further Reading   120

Introduction

Old (and Aristophanic) Comedy

Aristophanic comedy is not the sort of comedy with which we are familiar: situation comedy, comedy of errors and manners, plot and subplot, romance, with an emphasis on the familial and domestic. I would rather ask the reader to imagine a dramatic combination of the slapstick of the Three Stooges, the song and dance of a Broadway musical, the verbal wit of W. S. Gilbert or of a television show like *Frasier*, the exuberance of Mardi Gras, the open-ended plot line of *The Simpsons*, the parody of a Mel Brooks movie, the political satire of Doonesbury (or your favorite editorial cartoonist), the outrageous sexuality of *The Rocky Horror Picture Show*, and the fantasy of J. R. R. Tolkien, wrapped up in the format of a Monty Python movie.

Aristophanic comedy is "fantasy" or "farce" rather than pure "comedy." It depends not on complicated plot or subtle interaction of characters, but on the working out of a "great idea," the more bizarre the better (e.g., the sex-strike that stops the war in *Lysistrata*, or the establishment of Cloudcuckooland in *Birds*). Imagine a fantastic idea, wind it up and let it run, watch the logical (or illogical) conclusions that follow, and let the whole thing end in a great final scene. "Plot" is not a useful term here; of the eleven extant comedies of Aristophanes, only *Thesmophoriazusae* has anything like the linear plot of a modern comedy. The background is always topical and immediate, the city of Athens in the present, although in *Plutus* we can detect a shift from the local problems of Athens to those of Greece as a whole.

The comedy often features a central character—avoid the term "hero" here—who is responsible for the creation and execution of the great idea. Whitman attempted to create a type of "comic hero" in whose nature was a wide streak of *poneria* ("villainy"), but Aristophanes' heroes are not all cut from the same cloth. Some are old men (Dicaeopolis, Strepsiades, Trygaeus, Peithetaerus, Chremylus, "relative" in *Thesm.*); two are mature women (Lysistrata, Praxagora). In *Frogs* the protagonist is a god, Dionysus, a familiar character in comedy. In *Wasps* the great idea is devised by a younger man (Contracleon) for the good of his elderly and cantankerous father (Procleon), and the younger man has much in common with the poet. These protagonists stand up against a situation they find intolerable, create a brilliant and fanciful solution, and keep the comic pot bubbling to the end of the drama. Not all are wholly sympathetic; Strepsiades can be stupid and tiresome in the teaching scene with Socrates (*Cl.* 627–804), and more than one critic has seen Peithetaerus, the hero of *Birds*, as a comic portrait of megalomania.

Although Aristotle (*Poetics* 1447a35) knows of an etymology of "village song," comedy (*komoidia*) is "revel-song" (*komos* + *ode*), the celebration of exuberant release that was inherent in the worship of Dionysus. Songs and dancing must have been common to every Greek state, but formal comic drama is attested for Sicily in the early fifth century and then for Athens, where the genre would reach its greatest heights, in the fifth and fourth centuries.[1] As early as 330 B.C.E., Aristotle (*Ethics* 1128a 21–24) can distinguish "old" (*palaia*) comedy, where "indecency" (*aischrologia*, the closest the Greeks get to "obscenity") provided the humor, from "new" (*kaine*) comedy, where humor is derived by "innuendo" (*hyponoia*). Later in

---

[1] There are hints of something called "Megarian comedy," but whether the Megara meant is the city to the northwest of Athens or that in Sicily is uncertain (Aristotle *Poetics* 1448a29). Athenian comedians would make jokes at Megarian comedy as poor trash in comparison with their own—one such joke occurs at *Wasps* 56 ff., "you shouldn't expect anything too high-brow from us, but you're not going to get any of that disgusting stuff lifted off the Megarians either." It is uncertain whether this indicates a formal genre of comic drama at Megara.

the age of Alexandrian scholarship (the last three centuries B.C.E.), comedy was subdivided formally into a trinity of Old (*archaia*, although Aristotle's term *palaia* is sometimes found), Middle (*mese*), and New (*nea*). For Old Comedy the canonical starting date was 487–86, the first official state-sponsored production, while the death of Aristophanes in the late 380s provides a reasonable closing point. For New Comedy the début of its best known exponent, Menander (325 or 321), is a useful place to start. It is doubtful if "Middle Comedy" means anything more than "between Aristophanes and Menander" (i.e., c.380–c.320); it seems to be comedy in transition with no Aristophanes or Menander to dominate the comic stage.[2]

Old Comedy lasted for just about a hundred years, and thus what was first enacted in 487–86, or what Magnes, the first comedian about whom we know anything, produced for his victory in 472, is hardly going to be the same as what Aristophanes was creating at the end of the century. Old Comedy is not a monolithic art form, and Aristophanic comedy is not necessarily typical or perhaps even representative of Old Comedy. As I will outline, his comedy was very topical, "political" in the best sense of the word, but we can detect themes and subjects in the other Old Comic poets that are not to be found in Aristophanes. One such is the comic parody of myth. The best example here is Cratinus' lost *Dionysalexandros*, of which the hypothesis and some fragments remain; in this comedy Paris cannot be found to adjudicate his famous Judgment, and Dionysus must be pressed into service by Hermes. Aristophanes does not seem to have written this sort of comedy at the height of his career. He does write parody, but usually of specific tragedies by Euripides.[3] Or we find fragments in Pherecrates from comedies about women, domestic comedy, or the *hetaira*-play ("prostitute"). Aristophanes does write about women, but about women who have invaded the male public space. Only in his last two plays do we get

---

[2] For studies of Middle Comedy see W. G. Arnott, "From Aristophanes to Menander," *Greece & Rome* 19 (1972):65–80; H.-G. Nesselrath, *Die attische Mittlere Komödie* (Berlin 1990); and G. Dobrov (ed.), *Beyond Aristophanes* (Atlanta 1995).

[3] His *Phoenissae* ("Phoenician Women") is based on Euripides' late play of that title, and his *Lemniae* ("Women of Lemnos") on Euripides' *Hypsipyle* (also a late play).

women in domestic scenes. Aristotle tells us (*Poetics* 1449b7–9) that Crates (a contemporary of Aristophanes) "was the first to abandon the abusive style and write general plots," while another ancient source tells us that Pherecrates followed Crates in abstaining from personal abuse.[4] Thus it is clear that Old Comedy featured much more than the personal and political "satire" of Aristophanes, Eupolis, and Cratinus, but through the circumstances of survival we must depend on Aristophanes' eleven extant comedies for a play-length view of Old Comedy.

Aristophanes

We do not have biographies for ancient writers in the same way that a curious reader can open an encyclopedia and find the biographical details about Dante or Jane Austen or Tennessee Williams. There does exist a *Life of Aristophanes*, originating from the Alexandrian period, but it is hardly serious biography.[5] Rife with expressions such as "some say" or "according to others" that do not give the reader much confidence, most of the information is anecdotal and based on deductions (usually faulty) from what Aristophanes or other comedians have said in their plays. Every so often, however, we get an intriguing nugget that cannot be traced back to a comic source, for instance, the assertion that Plato sent Dionysius of Syracuse a copy of the plays of Aristophanes so that "he might learn about the government of Athens" (*Life* 42 ff.). We must use the *Life* with care, seeking material that does not seem to have come from comedy itself.

Similarly the *scholia* (ancient commentaries transmitted along with the comic texts) attempt to explain various references in Aristophanes, but on what evidence is uncertain, and the scholiasts have a strong tendency to be literally minded and to seek external and political compulsions on comedy.[6] There is also considerable

---

[4] Anon. *peri komodias* III (Koster):29–32.

[5] The Greek text of the *Life of Aristophanes* may be found at K-A III.2 nr. 1 (pp. 1–4), a translation at M. Lefkowitz, *The Lives of the Greek Poets* (London 1981), pp. 169–72. Lefkowitz argues (pp. 105–16) that the *Life* contains little of historical value.

[6] On the value of the comic scholia, especially for personal allusions, see S. Halliwell, "Ancient interpretations of ὀνομαστὶ κωμῳδεῖν in Aristophanes," *Classical Quarterly* 34 (1984):83–88.

information to be had from the various aspects of the later encyclopedic tradition (entries in the *Suda*, the lexicon of Photius, certain anonymous writers "on comedy"), and the ancient writers themselves have much to contribute, such as Plato's inclusion of Aristophanes in the company of his *Symposium* (c.380) or Aelian's story of Aristophanes' complicity in the "witch-hunt" against Socrates (*Varia Historia* 2.13). But again the evidence is of varying value.

All but one of the surviving comedies have come down with hypotheses that summarize the plays and provide intriguing details about the comedy and information about production; from the first hypothesis to *Birds*, for example, "it was produced in the archonship of Charias [415/4] at the City Dionysia through Callistratus; he was second with *Birds*, while Ameipsias won with *Komastai* ("Revellers"), and Phrynichus third with *Monotropos* ("The Hermit")." It is these that make possible the chronology listed below. Finally there are the comments of Aristophanes himself in the eleven plays that we have. These occur most often in the parabases (for which term see below), but also in the prologues and in certain choral interludes. From these we learn that Aristophanes had some connection with the island of Aegina (*Ach.* 652–54), made his comic début at an early age (*Cl.* 530), and could describe himself while no older than thirty as "the bald one" (*Peace* 767–74).

These last present a particular danger, however, in that there exists a great temptation to take Aristophanes at face value and to build a biography based on what he and other comedians allege. Much the same sort of thing happened with Roman poets such as Catullus, Propertius, and Ovid, whose personal poetry was used to reconstruct a biography of the poet's life without considering that we were being given the *persona* of a poet in love, not an accurate biographical picture. In the parabases of his first five plays, as well as in the prologues and at other points in the episodes and choral songs, Aristophanes gives us a picture of the young and innovative comic poet, and again this may be his face to the world rather than a real and accurate self-portrait. Obviously some truth must lurk beneath the comic front—Aristophanes and Cleon must have had some encounter in 426 and again later (cf. *Ach.* 377–82, 502 ff., 630 ff.; *Wasps* 1284–91), but we must not take the comedian as an impeccable source. We may think of modern comedians such as Jack Benny and Dean Martin, who propagated their self-myths of the miserly tightwad or the lovable drunk; Aristophanes cultivates the image of the unappreciated and brilliant artist. The biographical truth need not be the same.

The following biographical details can be accepted with reasonable confidence. Although there lurks a persistent tradition that he was charged on one or more occasions with *xenia* ("not being a citizen"), he was born an Athenian, son of Philippus, of the deme of Cydathenaeum. Attica was subdivided politically into 139 demes ("ridings," "parishes"), and Cydathenaeum was a wealthy city deme on the northwestern slopes of the Acropolis. Aristophanes' deme may indicate just that this was where his grandfather was living when the deme structure was put in place in the last years of the sixth century, but he clearly did have a good education and very likely belonged to the privileged classes. Although some have seen in his plays a real love of the countryside, as opposed to the *asty* ("town"), Aristophanes is very much a man of the city of Athens. His comedies are full of allusions to the people and issues and places of the city. Thus I can see him as a resident of this affluent city deme. Cydathenaeum was a deme of the tribe Pandionis. Thus, when the chorus at *Peace* 1173 describes a man seeing his name on the military list posted beside the statue of Pandion, we may detect a personal experience.

We should date his birth around the middle of the fifth century B.C.E. Some critics have interpreted *Clouds* 528 ff., referring to the production of his first play, *Banqueters*, in 427:

> It was here, in this very theatre,
> that my tale of the righteous boy and the little bugger was so very well
>   received.
> It is true that I was not yet of an age to mother properly such a child, and
>   so I exposed
> my prodigy to be adopted by another in my stead

as indicating that Aristophanes was not of legal age in 427, that is, younger than eighteen, and thus dated his birth c. 444. But this seems too literal a reading, and we should be content with a birthdate around 450; this would make him, incidentally, almost an exact contemporary of the infamous Alcibiades.[7]

---

[7] Cartledge, however, makes the interesting point (xvi) that on a birthdate of 444, Aristophanes would have come of age in 426, that same year as Cleon's first attack on him. Given the tradition of Aristophanes accused of *xenia*,

Aristophanes was one of four major figures of Old Comedy who came upon the scene in the 420s (Eupolis and Phrynichus in 429, Aristophanes in 427, Platon [not the philosopher] in 424). His dramatic career began in 427 with the production of his *Banqueters*. It enjoyed success, probably the second prize; if it had won, we would have expected Aristophanes to have trumpeted his success. His early plays (*Banqueters, Babylonians, Acharnians*) were all staged through other men as producers, Philonides and Callistratus, but this does not necessarily reflect his novice status. Aristophanes continued this practice, which is known for other poets, in his maturity (e.g., *Frogs* [405] through Philonides). His first comedy in his own name was *Knights* at the Lenaea of 424.

His early career has been the subject of considerable study in the last twenty-five years.[8] At the core of the debate is a passage from the parabasis of *Wasps* (1016–37) which was usually considered to suggest two stages in his early career as a poet: (i) "in secret, unseen, playing second fiddle to other dramatists" as indicating his comedies produced through others, i.e. 427–424L, and (ii) "then on that great day he ventured forth, alone into the fray, riding his own chariot of comedy" meaning his production of *Knights* at 424L; this will be picked up at 1029 "when he produced his own great plays." But others have made a plausible, if not totally persuasive, case for a three-fold division: (i) "in secret, unseen, playing second fiddle to other dramatists" as indicating his helping other poets *before* his own début in 427, (ii) "then on that great day he ventured forth . . ." as denoting his plays produced through others from 427–424, and (iii) a new stage indicated at 1029, "when he produced his own great plays," his "open" career beginning with *Knights* in 424. Another passage (*Kn.* 541–44) also suggests that Aristophanes saw his early career in more than two stages. On this reading Aristophanes will

---

Cartledge wonders if Cleon (of the same deme as Aristophanes) was making some trouble over the poet's citizenship as he came of age.

[8] See S. Halliwell, "Aristophanes' 'Apprenticeship,'" *Classical Quarterly* 30 (1980):33–45; D. Welsh, "*IG* ii² 2343, Philonides and Aristophanes' *Banqueters*," *Classical Quarterly* 33 (1983):51–55; N. W. Slater, "Aristophanes' apprenticeship again," *Greek, Roman and Byzantine Studies* 30 (1989):67–82; MacDowell (1995) chap. 3.

have cooperated with other poets and contributed to their comedies, and it gives an interesting glimpse of life behind the comic scenes.[9]

Two figures from his early career deserve mention. First there is Cleon, a political leader of the 420s, with whom the young poet seems to have two personal encounters and whom he attacks fiercely in several plays. Cleon has come down to us as the archdemagogue of late fifth-century Athens. Etymologically, "demagogue" is an inoffensive term (*demos* = "people" + *agein* = "lead"), but in both ancient Greek and modern English it acquired the pejorative overtones that "politician" possesses today. Cleon and his like were the "new men" of Athens in the 420s, members of the commercial middle class who had prospered during the period of Athenian supremacy, having made their money rather than inherited it, and who were seeking political power and challenging the authority of the traditional aristocratic leaders. In 426 Aristophanes put on his *Babylonians* at the Dionysia, and the three passages in *Acharnians* cited before plus the scholia *ad loc* show that Cleon took some official action against him, probably an *eisangelia* to the *Boule* (the Council of 500 that with the *ekklesia* ran the affairs of state) on the grounds of insulting the people in the presence of foreigners. The play turned in part, as far as we can gather from its meager remains, on the relationship between Athens and her allies ("the Cities").[10] It is equally likely that Aristophanes made fun of Cleon and that Cleon could not take a joke. The charge was probably

---

[9] The core of the debate is between G. Mastromarco, "L' esordio 'segreto' di Aristofane," *Quaderni di Storia* 5 (1979):153–92 and Halliwell (see note 8) against D. M. MacDowell, "Aristophanes and Kallistratos," *Classical Quarterly* 32 (1982):21–26 and F. Perusino, *Dalla commedia antica alla commedia di mezzo* (Urbino 1986). Slater, Sommerstein (*Wasps*) 215 ff., and S. Halliwell, "Authorial collaboration in the Athenian comic theatre," *Greek, Roman and Byzantine Studies* 30 (1989):515–28, pursue the tripartite division further.

[10] Many assumptions have been made concerning *Babylonians*, especially that Aristophanes was defending the allied cities against Athenian domination. On the play (which had Dionysus as a character) see MacDowell (1995), pp. 30–45, D. Welsh, "The chorus of Aristophanes' *Babylonians*," *Greek, Roman and Byzantine Studies* 24 (1983):137–50, and I. C. Storey, "The politics of 'angry Eupolis,'" *Ancient History Bulletin* 8 (1994):109–11.

rejected by the Council, but Aristophanes is very careful in *Acharnians* to stress that "I do not mean the city, just certain worthless individuals" (515 ff.). A second attack by Cleon took place in 423 and is reflected in some autobiographical lines in *Wasps* (1284–91), from which we can see that Aristophanes came to some agreement with Cleon (not to caricature him in comedy?), an agreement that he emphatically breaks in *Wasps*.[11] Cleon was one of Aristophanes' major targets in his comedy. *Knights* (424L) is a play-length attack on him, disguised thinly by the name "Paphlagon"; a section from the original version of *Clouds* (575–94) calls on the Athenians to "un-elect" Cleon as general; and he lurks beneath the whole of *Wasps*, in the names of the characters ("Procleon" and "Contracleon") and as a dog in the trial of the dogs (lines 891–1008).[12] His death in 422–21 effectively robbed the comedian of his favorite target. Hyperbolus, Cleon's successor as "leader of the people," was just not the same.

Then there is Eupolis, another of the new comedians of the 420s. A rather romantic picture has emerged of two young, new poets, friends and contemporaries arm in arm against the establishment, collaborators in the creation of new and sophisticated comedy.[13] Cratinus makes fun of Aristophanes for "using material from Eupolis" (fr. 213), and there seems to have been a public exchange in which Aristophanes accused Eupolis of plagiarizing his *Knights* in his *Maricas* (421L)—see *Cl.* 551–56—and Eupolis (fr. 89) retorted, "I helped the bald poet write those *Knights*, and made him a present of them." But all this comes from exchanges in comedy; Eupolis is a rival and a player in the great game involving poets and audiences. The rivalry and bitterness are probably thus overrated. The relationship between poets need not have been hostile and competitive, and one suspects that there is a great deal of

---

[11] See I. C. Storey, "*Wasps* 1284–91 and the portrait of Kleon in *Wasps*," *Scholia* 4 (1995):3–23.

[12] On the picture of Cleon in *Knights*, see L. Edmunds, *Cleon, Knights, and Aristophanes' Politics* (Lanham MD 1987); in *Wasps*, see Storey 1995.

[13] The testimonia and fragments of Eupolis at K–A V 294–539. See now I. C. Storey, *Eupolis, Poet of Old Comedy* (Oxford 2003).

intertextual material in the comedies that we simply just do not get.[14]

Aristophanes was credited with forty-four plays in antiquity, although four were attributed by the author of the *Life* to Archippus instead. Over a career of at least forty years he produced forty comedies, of which eleven have survived—the best survival rate of any Greek dramatist. The following dates can be presented with confidence—lost plays in [...]; the letters L and D designate the festival, Lenaea or Dionysia:

427	[*Daitales*]	"Banqueters"	2nd prize?
426D	[*Babylonioi*]	"Babylonians"	1st prize
425L	*Acharnes*	"Acharnians"	1st prize
424L	*Hippeis*	"Knights"	1st prize
423L	[play unknown]—see *Wasps* 1038		
423D	[*Nephelai*]	"Clouds"	3rd prize
422L	*Sphekes*	"Wasps"	2nd prize
	Proagon	"Preview"	1st prize[15]
421D	*Eirene*	"Peace"	2nd prize
c.418	*Nephelai*	"Clouds" [partly revised]	
414L	[*Amphiaraus*]		
414D	*Ornithes*	"Birds"	2nd prize
411L(?)	*Lysistrata*	"Lysistrata"	
411D(?)	*Thesmophoriazusae*	"Women at the Thesmophoria"	
408	[*Plutus*]	"Wealth"	
405L	*Batrachoi*	"Frogs"	1st prize
393-391	*Ecclesiazusae*	"Assembly-women"	
388	*Plutus*	"Wealth"	
after 388	[*Cocalus*][16]		
	[*Aiolosikon*]		

---

[14] Consult Halliwell (see note 9) and Hubbard on the relationship between the poets. K. Sidwell has also been advancing some interesting and controversial theories on the comic personae of the poets.

[15] The hypothesis to *Wasps* gives the second prize to Aristophanes' *Wasps* and the first to Philonides' *Proagon*, but Philonides is a known producer of Aristophanes' plays, and whenever *Proagon* is cited, it is attributed to Aristophanes. Aristophanes, it seems, found a way to win two prizes at the same festival.

[16] An inscription (*IG* ii2 2318.196) gives Araros a Dionysia-victory in 387; if the hypothesis to *Plutus* is correct that after 388 Aristophanes produced *Cocalus* and *Aiolosikon* through Araros, we can assign a victory with *Cocalus* to Aristophanes in 387.

Some of the lost plays can be dated to a year or so. For example, *Georgoi* ("Farmers") with its allusion to Nicias' behavior in 425 and a clear background of war (frr. 102, 111) must belong to the years 424–22, while *Holkades* ("Merchantships") is attested as a peace-play (Hypothesis I *Peace*) and as an attack on Cleon, thus also from the 420s—it *may* be the unknown comedy of 423L.

Aristophanes burst upon the scene with a vengeance. He may have hidden his light by assisting other poets before his début in 427, but from 427–21 he produced at least ten plays, an indication of this great new talent. He had his share of victories, at the Lenaea at least, inasmuch as we can identify victories at that festival in 425, 424, 422, and 405, but for the Dionysia things are less certain. An inscription (*IG* ii^2 2325.58) suggests strongly that he and then Eupolis won their first Dionysia-victories before 423; if his *Babylonians* did not win in 426, then he must have won at 425D. What I find peculiar is that we are never given a victory total for Aristophanes. For just about every other major poet of Old Comedy and also the "Big Three" of tragedy, we get victory totals; for example, for Eupolis, we get seven victories (of fourteen or fifteen plays), but for Aristophanes, silence. Is it possible that this greatest of Old Comic poets did not have an impressive victory total? We do know of four Lenaea-victories, but were these all there were? Perhaps the Dionysia-victory of 426 (or 425) was his only one, or one of just a few. He may have started off with several successes, perhaps enough to justify his claim at *Wasps* 1024 "And he won great honor, the likes of which had never before been awarded to any one man," but his later career may not have fulfilled these early expectations. Perhaps like Euripides, his reputation came later. Did Plato's attractive portrait of Aristophanes in *Symposium* make him the leading Old Comedian in the eyes of later antiquity?

About other details of his life we have little secure information. He seems not to have had a political career or to have held any elected office—here contrast Sophocles, the tragedian, who served Athens in a number of public capacities. An Aristophanes of Cydathenaeum is known to have served as a *bouleutes* (member of the Council of 500) early in the fourth century,[17] but this was not an elected magistracy. This may be our Aristophanes, or conceivably a

---

[17] See B. D. Meritt and J. S. Traill, *The Athenian Agora: vol. XV, Inscriptions: The Athenian Councillors* (Princeton 1974) nr. 12, pp. 32 ff.

grandson. In 405 his *Frogs*, produced at the height of his career and just months before the war would end disastrously for Athens, won a crown of leaves from the sacred olive tree and the unprecedented honor of a second production; this was due, according to Dicaearchus, to the parabasis.[18]

He had three sons, Araros, Philippus, and a third whose name is given variously as Philetaerus or Nicostratus.[19] They are all described as comic poets, but only Araros seems to have made any mark, and if Alexis fr. 184 is to believed, he did not live up to his father ("I have a very deep well inside, more frigid than the comedy of Araros"). Aristophanes is said to have produced his last two plays, *Cocalus* and *Aiolosikon*, through Araros (Hypothesis IV *Plutus*). His last play in his own name was *Plutus* (388), and we know of the two produced through his son. Thereafter Aristophanes disappears from view, and we may reasonably date his death in the period 385–80. Plato's *Symposium* dates from about 380, and if Aristophanes had died in the recent past, the brilliant picture created by Plato may be seen as a posthumous tribute to him. Webster thought that an elegant grave relief of a comic poet dating to the late 380s might be that of Aristophanes, but more recent opinion dates this relief to the middle of the century, too late to be that of Aristophanes.[20]

Comic Festivals and Production

Comedy, along with the older dramatic genres of tragedy and satyr-play, was produced at public festivals in honor of the god Dionysus. Too often we think of Dionysus as "jolly Bacchus," whom the Romans in particular portrayed as the god of drinking and sexual orgies. But he was far more, a god of the dark side of humanity, of passions and the life force, companion of the Mother, a dying and rising god of the year cycle, god of the mountain rather than the city,

---

[18] *Life* 32–39 and Hypothesis I *Frogs*. The date of the restaging of *Frogs* has been the subject of much recent discussion. See Sommerstein (*Frogs*), 21.

[19] For the testimonia and fragments see K–A II 524–31 (Araros), VII 322–32 (Philetaerus), VII 353–5 (Philippus), VII 74–92 (Nicostratus).

[20] See T. B. L. Webster, *Monuments Illustrating Old and Middle Comedy*, BICS Supp. 39, 3rd ed. (London 1978), p. 117.

whose followers were mainly male satyrs and female maenads ("the mad women"), who dressed in animal skins, wreathed their hair with ivy, wielded *thyrsoi* (poles tipped with foliage), hunted their prey on the mountainside, tore it apart, and ate the flesh raw.[21] Euripides' *Bacchae* (c.407) gives the best picture of this god and his rites as seen through fifth-century eyes. His main festival at Athens was the City Dionysia, held in late March or early April. A "city" Dionysia may seem like a contradiction in terms, and what the Athenians seem to have done is to tame Dionysus by diverting the wild festivals more suited to the mountain to a context within the city. And part of this worship was drama, in part perhaps the replacement of the savage reality with a controlled reenactment.

The canonical date for the beginning of Old Comedy is 487–86 (*Suda* χ 318, s.v. Chionides), that is, the first formal inclusion of comedy at the City Dionysia. This was the major festival of Dionysus and of the dramas produced in his honor, but from the late 440s comedies were staged formally at the Lenaea also, a festival in late January or early February.[22] Tragedies also were performed at the Lenaea, but this was comedy's festival. There is some evidence that the Lenaea was a lesser festival; an ancient source speaks of Platon "being bumped back to the Lenaea" after a fourth-place finish at the Dionysia, but this may just be a faulty deduction by the ancient source.[23]

For the Dionysia, we know that it lasted five days, 10–14 Elaphebolion, that the first day was devoted to the formal parade (*pompe*) of the god, and that contests for tragedy, comedy, and dithyrambs (songs with a chorus of fifty) took place during these days. The exact order of events is in dispute, but a reasonable reconstruction is found in Csapo and Slater (103–8): Day 1 —*pompe* + dithyrambs; Day 2—five comedies, one by each poet; Day 3—three

---

[21] On the cult of Dionysus see E. R. Dodds, *Euripides' Bacchae* (Oxford 1960), and R. Seaford, *Euripides Bacchae* (Warminster 1996).

[22] For translations of and commentary on the ancient evidence see Csapo and Slater, pp. 103–85.

[23] *P.Oxy.* 2737, fr. i, col. ii 1–17 says that Platon did well when he produced through others, but when he produced *Rhabdouchoi* ("Theater Police") on his own, he finished fourth and was bumped back to the Lenaea; see Csapo and Slater nr. 71.

tragedies + satyr-play by a tragedian; Day 4—three tragedies + satyr-play by the second tragedian; Day 5—three tragedies + satyr-play by the third tragedian. Five comedies are attested for the years 434 and 388, but the hypotheses to several of Aristophanes' comedies list only three prizes. It has often been assumed that during the war the comedies were reduced from five to three, and that they followed the tragedians, one on each of days 3 to 5. But this was challenged by Luppe and others, and the number may have remained at five throughout.[24] The passage at *Birds* 786–89 about flying off during a boring tragedy and then flying "back in plenty of time to see us" does not have to refer to comedy; it just means "to the theatre."[25]

These occasions were religious festivals; drama was part of the ritual ceremonies of the god, and several recent critics have read the comedies with a ritual subtext.[26] But even more significant is that they were public and civic occasions. There was a political side to the festivals. One of the nine archons was responsible for each of the dramatic contests; poets were "granted choruses" by that official, a *misthos* ("stipend") was paid to the poet, and a *choregos* ("sponsor") appointed to pick up the costs of production as part of his public responsibility ("liturgy"). These were state-sponsored productions, and considerable debate attends the question of why the Athenian democracy ran these dramatic festivals essentially at state expense. Especially at the City Dionysia the role of the city loomed large—no public business was transacted, the ten elected generals would enter formally and pour the opening libation, the *phoros* ("tribute") from the cities would be paraded formally through the theatre, benefactors of the city would be honored, and those whose fathers had died in battle would receive a suit of armor from the city when they came of age.[27] Theatres in ancient Greece were large—that at

---

[24] W. Luppe, "Die Zahl der Konkurrenten an den komischen Agonen zur Zeit des peloponnischen Krieges," *Philologus* 116 (1972):53–76; against this view see G. Mastromarco, "Guerra peloponnesiaca e agoni comici in Atene," *Belfagor* 30 (1975):469–73. See also Csapo and Slater 107 and Storey 2002.

[25] See Dunbar (*Birds*), p. 481.

[26] See Storey 1992: 3 ff.

[27] See Csapo and Slater, p. 107 ff., and an important study by S. Goldhill, "The Great Dionysia and Civic Ideology," *Journal of Hellenic Studies* 107 (1987):58–76.

Athens is estimated to have held fifteen thousand to seventeen thousand spectators—and thus the tragedies and comedies played to the state as audience. Drama was not the province of a few in a covered theatre; it was for the people as a larger body. We need to imagine a combination of the faithful gathered in Vatican Square on Easter Day, the crowds that fill the Mall on the Fourth of July, and the audiences on the opening night of a great summer blockbuster. Drama was intensely alive and intensely important to the people of Athens.

We are used to "theatre of illusion"—the three-sided box and special effects make us believe that we are there, watching what goes on. But Greek drama is "theatre of convention," or, in Taplin's phrase, "theatre of the mind." The audience will do a great deal of the work in allowing the drama (tragic or comic) to work. Notice the opening of Menander's *Dyskolos* (the speaker is the god Pan):

Imagine the setting to be Phyle in Attica, and the shrine that I am coming out of is that of the people of Phyle . . . a well-known place. In the house on the right lives Knemon, a thoroughly unpleasant man . . .

The audience is told in the prologue what the program notes provide today.

The theatrical space in the time of Aristophanes was located on the southeastern slope of the Acropolis, in an area that had long been sacred to Dionysus (Thuc. 2.15.4). All one really needs for a Greek theatre is a hill and a flat space at the bottom, a circular dancing-place (*orchestra*) for the chorus, and an acting-space for the actors.[28] Aristophanes operated with a flat *orchestra* (about sixty-five feet across), two passages from each side that allowed the entrance of chorus and actors (*eisodoi*), and a stage building (*skene* = "tent," "shack") with at least one door. The flat roof of this building could also be used for scenes above ground level—at *Wasps* 68 Contracleon is "sleeping up there on the roof." Certain scenes from comedy show that there was a window in the *skene* so that actors inside could be seen and heard outside (e.g., Procleon's appearance at *Wasps* 155–70).

---

[28] The physical aspect is well presented for the student by Csapo and Slater, pp. 79–88, and by G. Ley, *A Short Introduction to the Ancient Greek Theater* (Chicago 1991). A more technical study is that of Dearden.

Two points are the subject of debate: the number of doors and the presence of a low stage in front of the *skene*. By the time of Menander's *Dyskolos* (317) there are clearly three doors in the *skene*-building, but this play postdates the great rebuilding of the theatre by Lycurgus in the third quarter of the fourth century. Critics claim that certain scenes demand more than one door, but given the minimalist nature of the Greek theatre, the audience would not be bothered when the door changed its identity within a comedy.[29] In *Frogs* a single door could be that of Heracles' house and later the entry to the palace of Hades. There is good humor also to be had from a single door representing two houses, for example, the houses of Lamachus and Dicaeopolis at *Ach.* 1069–1142 as delicacies are brought out for the latter and the items of war for the former. But there are places where two doors seem to be needed, for example, at *Cl.* 125 where Pheidippides says "I'm going inside" and then Strepsiades proceeds to knock at the door of Socrates' Pondertorium. A similar staging is needed at lines 800 ff. *Wasps* and *Birds*, on the other hand, can be played with a single door throughout.

The matter of the raised stage is equally problematic. Ewans and Wiles insist that the focus of the playing-space is the center of the orchestra, where an altar was placed, which could be used in the play (at *Thesm.* 689 ff., Euripides' kinsman takes refuge from the women), or the line connecting that center to the main door, and that a raised stage is useless in a high theatre where much of the audience is well above the playing-area.[30] But there are indications in the text of a raised area, for instance, at *Kn.* 149 "come up here," and vase-paintings of comic scenes do show a raised structure.[31] If there was a "stage," it was low and provided no impediment to the actors operating in the orchestra and interacting with the chorus or even with the audience.

Physical effects are not prominent in the Greek theatre. The *skene*

---

[29] See Dearden, pp. 20–30.

[30] M. Ewans, *Aischylos. The Oresteia* (London 1995), xx–xxii (esp. n. 14 for bibliography); D. Wiles, *Tragedy in Performance* (London 1997) chap. 3.

[31] See Taplin plates 9.1, 11.3, 12.5, 12.6, 14.12, 15.13. These are from the fourth century, and thus later than the plays that inspired the vase-painters; they may reflect the presence of a stage in fourth-century Italian comedy or just be a convention to communicate the fact that this is a dramatic performance.

could be painted or decorated to suit its use as a palace, house, cave, or temple, and the opening scene of *Wasps* shows that a net has been placed over the front and that the door has been barred. For special effects there was the *ekkyklema* ("roll-out"), which was some sort of wheeled platform allowing an interior scene or tableau to be displayed. The most famous instances are in Aeschylus' *Oresteia*, where first Clytemnestra and then Orestes are shown standing over the bodies of their victims, but in comedy the students inside Socrates' Pondertorium are so displayed at 185 ff., and two tragic poets, Euripides and Agathon, are wheeled out in the process of composition at *Ach.* 409 and *Thesm.* 96. Then there is the *mechane*, a cranelike device that would allow actors to hover in the air and deliver their lines or to swing from behind to the front of the *skene*. The most striking example is the opening of *Peace* where Bellerophon's famous ride to Olympus on Pegasus is transformed into an elderly Athenian riding the world's largest dung-beetle, but it is also used for the entry of Socrates at *Cl.* 218, suspended in some fashion from the crane.

Props in tragedy are rare, and when they occur, for instance, the purple carpet in *Agamemnon*, or the bow of Heracles in Sophocles' *Philoctetes*, they are significant items. Comedy uses physical items much more often; the austerity of tragedy is definitely lacking. *Wasps* in particular is a very visual comedy—we have the house besieged at the start, the chorus costumed as Wasps, the creation of a trial space at home with all the necessary paraphernalia, the procession of the household vessels, and the dressing-up of father in fine cloak and elegant footwear.

A rule of three actors seems to have operated for both tragedy and comedy.[32] It is usually assumed that it was an external restriction, designed to assure a level playing-field among competitors, and for the most part Aristophanic comedy can be performed with three actors only. Sometimes there seem to be four speaking parts, for example, in the scene with the ambassadors at *Birds* 1565–1693 (Peithetaerus, Poseidon, Heracles, and the Triballian), but the last speaks only three lines of pidgin Greek (1615, 1628, 1678), and these would be spoken by one of the other actors. Actors took multiple

---

[32] See D. M. MacDowell, "The Number of Speaking Actors in Old Comedy," *Classical Quarterly* 44 (1994):325–35, and C. W. Marshall, "Comic Technique and the Fourth Actor," *Classical Quarterly* 47 (1997):77–84.

roles, for instance in *Clouds* the actors playing Strepsiades and Socrates play the two *Logoi*, and in *Birds* Euelpides is given a formal sendoff at 846–50, because his actor is needed for other parts in the episodes. In a theatre with fifteen thousand spectators and with masked actors, it would be difficult for a spectator to discern who was speaking in a multiple scene; hence three-actor scenes need to be well choreographed and the roles sharply distinguished.

The costumes of the comic actors were bizarre, intended to be ridiculous—Aristotle (*Poet.* 1449a33) identifies *to geloion* ("the ridiculous") as the aim of comedy—involving grotesque masks, padding of shoulders, paunch, and buttocks, and a dangling phallus. Taplin has some instructive illustrations of the comic actor— that of the intriguing "*Choregoi*" vase shows both comic and tragic actors on stage.[33] The difference in dress and mask is arresting.

Tragic choruses had twelve members, whereas comedy seems to have had twice that number. The prominence of the chorus in fifth-century drama suggests that Aristotle was right to trace both tragedy and comedy to choral performances, from which actors gradually spun off. The archon's phrase for accepting a poet's submission was "to grant a chorus," and for much of the fifth century a chorus is a necessary part of the drama, although in the tragedies of Euripides we sometimes feel its marginality. In comedy, however, the chorus has an essential role. The chorus can oppose or support the great idea and its proponent. It can also carry much of the imagery of the drama. In *Clouds* the chorus provides imagery for lofty, insubstantial ideas; in two other plays, it may represent old jurors with a sting (*Wasps*) or the flight of fancy that creates Cloudcuckooland (*Birds*). It can speak for the poet on various occasions, as well as provide a song-and-dance to fill the interludes. Only in the latter two plays does the chorus begin to lose its importance, and the breaks between scenes are now filled in the manuscripts and papyri with <*chorou*> ("of the chorus"), that is, with songs not written for the occasion. By the time of Menander and the development of the five-act structure, the chorus comes on stage only to fill the gaps and has no dramatic or thematic role in the comedy. Sometimes we get double choruses, as in *Lysistrata* where

---

[33] See Taplin plates 9.1 (the "*Choregoi*" vase), 10.2, 11.3, 11.4, 12.5, 12.6 (particularly expressive), and 16.16.

two half-choruses oppose each other (old women versus old men) and in Eupolis' lost *Maricas* (421L) where half-choruses of rich and poor each champion a political antagonist. The chorus is usually a homogenous body, but we do have places where each *choreutes* could have been individually represented (and costumed), such as the twenty-four different birds at *Birds* 297–304 and the chorus in Eupolis' lost *Poleis* where the *choreutai* were twenty-four cities of the empire.

The festivals were also competitions; prizes were given for the best comic poet and for the best actor. Thus to the atmosphere described before we might perhaps add the excitement of Oscar night. Judges were selected from each of the ten tribes; five of these votes were selected at random, and the decision made on this basis. Thus the festivals would be rife with the spirit of competition and rivalry, and often we get hints of the great game involving poets, rivals, judges, and audience, as in the prologue of *Wasps*:

> Now you shouldn't expect anything too highbrow from us . . . what
> we've got here is just a little story, but with a moral,
> something we can all understand. Don't worry, it won't go
>   over your heads,
> but it will still be on a higher level than those other disgusting,
>   obscene farces.   (56, 64–66)

Or see the second parabases of *Clouds* (1116–30) and *Birds* (1102–17) where the chorus threatens and cajoles the judges for a favorable verdict. One of the best exchanges took place in 424 and 423 when Aristophanes made fun of his competitor, Cratinus, as a drunken old playwright, well past his prime (*Kn.* 526–36), and Cratinus responded with his *Pytine* at 423D, in which he put himself into his own play, as the poet who had deserted his true wife, Comedy, for another woman, Pytine or "the Wine Flask." The revised parabasis of *Clouds* (518–62) shows Aristophanes' reaction to his third-place finish that year—and like the woman in Hamlet's play, I think he "doth protest too much."

The extant remains of the Theatre of Dionysus show an elaborately paved marble floor, well-cut marble seats, and a high raised stage, but all this is postclassical. In the fifth century the orchestra was flat earth, and the seats wooden benches (*tu ikria*). The audience consisted principally, but not exclusively, of Athenian male citizens; the resident-aliens (*metoikoi*) attended at both festivals, and *xenoi* and allies from the cities were certainly present at the Dionysia. Boys were in the audience, but could women attend? This has been the subject of much discussion, with much of the evidence coming from comedy itself.[34] The debate rests on the dominant nature of the dramatic festival; if it were primarily a religious occasion, why would the women be barred from this one festival only, when women were so involved in the religious life of the city? But if drama is essentially a civic occasion, then women as noncitizens might well have been excluded or strongly discouraged. Perhaps the question is not "could women attend?" but "did women attend?" Perhaps the presence of women was a class-based matter, with the upper classes more secluded than the women who lived and worked in the agora. But Henderson is certainly right that whether women were there in any numbers, "the notional audience was male." Thus at *Peace* 51–53 the servant announces, "And I will explain the plot to the kids, to the young men, and the grown men, to the important men, and to the super-important men over there." The audience is thought of and addressed as "gentlemen," not as "ladies and gentlemen." One major difference between tragedy and comedy lies in its relationship to the audience.[35] Tragedy very rarely admits its own existence and does not call attention to itself—this is frequently referred to as "meta-theatre"—whereas comedy does all it can to destroy the theatrical illusion. Comedy pulls its audience into the drama, both in the direct addresses in the prologue and the parabasis and in such scenes as at *Clouds* 1094 ff., where Superior Argument, invited to look at the audience, agrees that the perverts are in the majority.

Structure of an Old Comedy

The eleven plays of Aristophanes display certain common structural features that seem also to occur in the fragments of the other

---

[34] Three articles take differing stances: A. Podlecki, "Could Women Attend the Theater in Ancient Athens?" *Ancient World* 21 (1990):27–43; J. Henderson, "Women in the Athenian Dramatic Festivals," *Transactions of the American Philological Association* 121 (1991):133–47; and S. Goldhill, "Representing Democracy: Women at the Great Dionysia," in R. Osborne and S. Hornblower, eds., *Ritual, Finance, Politics* (Oxford 1994):347–69. See also Csapo and Slater, pp. 286–93, for the ancient evidence.

[35] See O. Taplin, "Fifth-century Tragedy and Comedy: a *synkrisis*," *Journal of Hellenic Studies* 106 (1986):163–74.

comedians. Clearly the poets and their audience expected certain repeated and familiar features in comedy, but Aristophanes (and presumably his rivals as well) varies these features so much that there is no "typical" or "normal" comedy among the extant eleven. It is fair, however, to say that *Knights* and *Wasps* come the closest to a standard form.[36]

1. **Prologue:** Comedy, unlike tragedy, has to create and introduce its own plots and characters, and also must warm up its audience for a sympathetic and favorable reception. Prologues usually run for two hundred or so lines, and thus consist of several scenes, and can include singing by the actors. The meter is the usual iambic trimeter ("the closest to ordinary speech"—Aristotle *Poetics* 1449a25). In *Clouds* the prologue consists of a scene where the father complains of his son's ruinous debts (1–125), the entry to and pageant of the students at the Pondertorium (126–217), and Strepsiades' first encounter with Socrates (218–74).

2. **Parodos:** This is the entry of the chorus.[37] The identity of the chorus is usually divulged in the prologue (as at *Wasps* 214–29) so that the audience will have some idea of what to expect. The chorus may enter to assist the main character (as in *Knights*, *Peace*, *Plutus*), or to oppose him (as in *Acharnians*, *Wasps*, *Birds*, and the chorus of old men in *Lysistrata*); sometimes they watch and observe (as in *Frogs*). This section is sung, that is, it tends to be in lyric meter rather than in the iambic trimeters so prevalent elsewhere. The entry of the chorus must have been one of the awaited moments of the play. Its members can rush violently onstage, ready to do battle (*Ach.*, *Kn.*), but *Clouds*, *Wasps*, and *Birds* show interesting variations. The chorus members of *Wasps* can barely walk, let alone rush onstage; they have also a supporting chorus of boys. In *Birds* the spectacle is the wonderful variation of bird costumes and the choreography; there must have been the same gush of enthusiasm as when the curtain rises on a particularly gorgeous set in the theatre. In *Clouds*

---

[36] The fullest study of comic structure is in A.W. Pickard Cambridge, *Dithyramb, Tragedy, and Comedy*, 2nd ed. (Oxford 1962), pp. 194–229; Sommerstein (*Ach.*) 9–11 has a useful summary.

[37] See Zimmermann on the parodos.

Aristophanes plays games with the audience; for instance, Strepsiades cannot see the Clouds until they are "there, in the wings!" (326)—comedy again calling attention to itself. As with the prologue, the parodos may consist of a string of scenes.

3. **Agon:** Often the comedy will turn on the result of a formal contest between two speakers, the agon.[38] A symmetrical pattern exists in the agon, for each side outlines his or her argument. The chorus sets the terms; with the *agon* in *Clouds* as a model, they begin with a song (ode—949–56), then introduce the first speaker (959–60), who then states his case in a tetrameter (usually anapestic or iambic),[39] with interjections by opponent, chorus, or a third party (961–1010). The first speaker ends with a *pnigos* ("choking-song"— 1011–23), in which the tetrameter is cut in half to a dimeter. The same format is repeated for the second side: antode (same metrical pattern as the ode—1025–32), introduction (1034–5), second speaker (tetrameter—1036–84), *pnigos* (1085–1100). Some plays contain two formal agons (*Knights* and *Clouds*), some have the formal pattern, but only one speaker who outlines his case in an exposition (*Birds, Eccl.*); three plays lack an agon of the formal sort just outlined (*Ach., Peace, Thesm.*—they do have important speeches by the main character, and, interestingly enough, the first and last are concerned with tragedy). In *Frogs* the structure is inverted, the episodes coming before the agon, and the agon itself (between Euripides and Aeschylus) does not resolve the larger contest. When there is a formal debate, the second speaker is the victor, except for *Plutus* where Penia ("Poverty") speaks second and should win, but the play proceeds with the first speaker victorious. Much scholarly blood has been spilled in the debate whether this means that the comedy should be taken as ironic rather than as straight fantasy.[40]

---

[38] Gelzer (1960) is the standard study of the comic agon.

[39] The anapestic tetrameter catalectic is a more elegant and loftier meter, the iambic tetrameter catalectic more down-to-earth and informal; in *Clouds* the older antagonist (Superior Argument) speaks in anapests, whereas his modern counterpart (Inferior) uses iambics. The same thing happens in *Frogs*, Aeschylus (anapests) v. Euripides (iambics).

[40] For a good summary of the problem and a controversial interpretation see A. H. Sommerstein, "Aristophanes and the Demon Poverty," *Classical Quarterly* 34 (1984):314–33. MacDowell (1995) 292 doubts whether the

4. **Parabasis:** This is perhaps the most curious and formal feature of Old Comedy. It is sung by the chorus with the actors offstage, directed to the audience, and comes at a natural break in the action, often just before or just after an agon. As with the agon, a formal pattern can be detected, although Aristophanes' parabases vary from comedy to comedy. The full structure is best found in the parabases of *Clouds*, *Wasps*, and *Birds*. I will use the first as a model: [a] song, often directed to the departing actors (510–16); [b] parabasis proper (518–62), in a fifteen-syllable meter, most commonly the anapestic tetrameter catalectic,[41] although in *Clouds* Aristophanes sharpens his attack on other poets by usurping the eupolidean meter of his rival Eupolis; [c] a *pnigos* in the same meter, reduced to a dimeter; this rounds off the parabasis proper (563–74); [d] ode (not found in *Clouds*); [e] epirrhema (575–94)—an address (probably by the chorus leader) to the audience, usually in trochaic tetrameter catalectic or the rarer paeonic tetrameter (*Wasps* 1275–83); [f] antode (595–604); [g] antepirrhema (607–26). The last four, [d]–[g], are known collectively as the "epirrhematic syzygy," and can be found on their own without [a]–[c]; this happens in *Frogs* where the anapests of [b] occur in the parodos at 354–71 and the syzygy in the break at 674–737, and also in second parabases (see following).

Not all plays have parabases with such a neat format. In *Ach.* the song [a] is reduced to a pair of anapestic tetrameters; in *Peace* we get only [b] + [c], and the ode/antode [d] + [f]; in *Lysist.* with its two semichoruses, the parabasis takes the form of two syzygies, with no parabasis proper. *Thesm.* has a very stripped-down parabasis, possessing [b] + [c] and only one epirrhema [f]. There is no formal parabasis in *Eccl.* or *Plutus*.

The chorus sometimes speaks of "stripping off for our anapests" (*Ach.* 627); this may be meant metaphorically, but if the parabasis were accompanied by vigorous dancing, it may well have removed outer cloaks for this purpose. The chorus stays in its character (as wasps or birds), except for the parabasis proper and *pnigos* of the first five extant comedies, where the chorus becomes

---

audience were even aware of Aristophanes' technique of the second speaker's winning; this I do not find convincing.

[41] The anapestic tetrameter catalectic was in fact called the "aristophanean" by the ancients.

the poet himself, developing his comic persona (the young, brilliant, and unappreciated poet), praising his own art, running down his rivals, and tweaking the audience for their lack of support. But in *Birds* the chorus members are birds throughout. In the syzygy of the principal parabasis the chorus reverts to (or maintains) its dramatic role, explaining why jurors should be wasps or what clouds and birds can do for humanity.

It is frequently supposed that these formal and repeated features indicate that the parabasis is an old element in comedy, dating from the early history of comedy. Aristophanes and his contemporaries may well have found the parabasis as an established and expected feature of comedy, but studies by Bowie and Hubbard have demonstrated that it is thematically essential to the play and not just a venerable appendage maintained by conservatively minded poets for a similarly traditional audience.[42]

5. **Episodes:** These are scenes dominated by the actors, normally in iambic trimeter, but interspersed with choral elements. Very often they follow the agon and reveal the dramatic consequences of the great idea. The best of these, perhaps the best scene in all Aristophanes, is the trial of the dogs in *Wasps* (891–1008) which proceeds from Contracleon's victory in the agon and the decision to try cases at home. In the second half of comedies such as *Ach.*, *Peace*, *Birds*, *Eccl.*, and *Plutus* we get series of "intruders" who enter to be part of the great idea now implemented and who are usually driven off with slapstick violence. *Frogs* is an interesting exception, in that the episodes precede the agon and occupy the first half of the comedy. What can be observed is how Aristophanes varies these scenes with great finesse; in *Birds* we get three distinct sets of episodes which might stretch out this longest of extant comedies, but they succeed admirably in maintaining the interest and attention of the audience.

6. **Choral songs (*kommatia*):** The episodes are separated by choral interludes in which the chorus may address the audience again or engage in extended personal humor. Some in fact are parabatic in form and are usually described as "second" parabases (*Cl.* 1116–30, *Wasps* 1265–91—this lacks the antode—and *Birds*

---

[42] Hubbard passim; A. M. Bowie, "The Parabasis in Aristophanes: Prolegomena, *Acharnians*," *Classical Quarterly* 32 (1982):27–40.

1058–1117); *Ach.* has a second and even a third parabasis (971–99, 1143–72). One particular sequence deserves note: the trochaic songs at *Birds* 1470–92, 1553–64, 1694–1705, where the chorus of birds reflects on certain strange sights who turn out to be notorious denizens on the Athenian scene.

7. **Exodos:** The formal conclusion to the play. Aristophanes' plays end in a number of ways: reconciliation of the semichoruses in *Lysistrata*, the marriages in *Peace* and *Birds*, the party at the end of *Acharnians*, the sense of victory and general rejoicing in *Knights* and *Frogs*. Two endings are worth mentioning: the dancing contest at the close of *Wasps* where the old man dances all contenders into oblivion, including the actual figures of Carcinus and his sons (the poet claims that he is the first to send a chorus off dancing), and the finale of *Clouds* where the entire action of the comedy is reversed with the burning down of Socrates' Pondertorium. Such a "down" ending is rare and must be explained by the revision of the play. In any case, the *exodos* must have been the equivalent of the final number that climaxes a Broadway musical or a Gilbert & Sullivan operetta.

Interpreting Aristophanes

Aristophanes is a challenging poet for critics, and the twentieth century has seen much debate over how we should appreciate his comedies. The fundamental question is, "How serious is Aristophanes?" He makes fun of people and institutions, of issues and ideas; it is often assumed, and not just by students coming to Aristophanes for the first time, that if he makes fun of someone (or something), he must be opposed to it, that he is making a statement; in short, his comedy is satire or propaganda. This was how critics in the early part of the century approached Aristophanes—he was writing from a certain viewpoint and aiming to get that point across. The problem was that whatever standpoint was accepted (partisan of peace, champion of the people or of country folk or of city dwellers, conservative traditionalist), one had to ignore other parts of his comedy to make one's case.[43] Perhaps the extreme instance of

---

[43] Whitman, chap. 1, has a very good summary of such early views of Aristophanes.

this approach was Norwood's (210) suggestion that Cleon's rivals had suborned Aristophanes to write his *Knights* against Cleon.

The poles of the debate about comedy versus satire/propaganda are the studies of Gomme and de Ste Croix. The former argues in a landmark article that Aristophanes is serious only about his art, that his claim to be a new and sophisticated poet is what we should take at face value, that there is very little that is serious politically in his comedy. Gomme provided a useful corrective to the theory that comedy is essentially propaganda, and his thesis that we should give primacy to his claims as a comic poet led to several good studies during the 1950s and 1960s of comic structure and fantasy. In 1972 de Ste Croix provided the counterpoint to Gomme; while not denying the primacy of humor, he argued that a comedian may also be serious, that we should seek passages where there is no obvious humor, where we seem to glimpse the poet behind his plays, and that what he finds funny (in the case of *Wasps*, the jury system itself) is also significant. His conclusion was that a "Cimonian" bias could be found behind Aristophanes' comedy, that is, a conservative right-of-center leaning that favored traditional values and leaders and that may have been democratic, but endorsed a democracy firmly led by the *kaloi k'agathoi* ("the good and noble"). This approach has won several adherents, most notably Sommerstein (1996), who has formed the same conclusion from a study of the *komodoumenoi* ("the people made fun of"); Edmunds, who in his study of *Knights* assumes a political crusade by the poet; MacDowell ("Aristophanes is not just trying to make the Athenians laugh but is making a serious point which is intended to influence them" [1995] p. 6); and Henderson (in Winkler & Zeitlin 1990), for whom Old Comedy was a sort of "unofficial opposition" to the democracy of the day.

Not all critics accept comedy as political satire. In the past fifteen years several other approaches have been followed, often dealing with *Acharnians*, where Aristophanes openly identifies himself with the main character on two occasions (377–82, 502 ff.) and the play is often read as an earnest plea for peace in 425. Heath argues that comedy was *never* taken seriously, either politically or even when Aristophanes makes claims about his comedy. Goldhill points to the many "voices" in a comedy, to the many stances and attitudes a comedian must adopt; how can one argue that one is the genuine Aristophanes that must take precedence over the rest? Carrière and Halliwell pay great attention to the cultural theories of Bakhtin, on which comedy is essentially "carnival," a release from the ordinary life of the city, and that it should not be taken as serious politics, but as the fulfilment of wish and escapism. Bowie has developed what has become a popular modern interpretation, ritual as a subtext for comedy, for instance, *Wasps* as a parody of the *ephebeia* (the coming of age of young men); the audience would appreciate the reversal of roles inherent in the concept. Taaffe and Muecke have brought feminist techniques into play in the plays of gender confusion (*Lysist., Thesm., Eccl.*), while Reckford downplays the importance of politics in comedy in favor of the healing powers of laughter and comedy.[44]

A safe middle ground needs to be found by the student trying to cope with this intensely topical comedy. One needs to resist the temptation that making fun of someone or something is the same as trying "to get" that target. Humor does not necessarily have to have a bite. On the other hand, de Ste Croix is quite right to insist that comedy can be serious, and the evidence adduced (the parabasis of *Frogs*, Lysistrata's speech at 1112–56, the return to the golden days of the past in the closing scenes of *Knights*, the frequent barbs at the jury system that was one of the pillars of the democracy, the attacks on the demagogues while politicians of traditional background are spared) is impressive. But another question can be raised: Does comedy lead or follow public opinion? The demagogues (Cleon, Cleophon, Hyperbolus, and their ilk) are caricatured with little mercy, but in the 420s they were a novelty and thus a comedian's dream. They were the natural target for the comic poet and his audience; Aristophanes' caricature of them may owe more to public taste than to political or personal animosity. The same may be said of the familiar antithesis in comedy of old = good/modern = bad (cf. the end of *Knights* and *Lysistrata* or the parabasis of *Frogs*); the poet may be giving vent to his own deeply held feelings or just catering to popular taste.

---

[44] M. Heath, *Political Comedy in Aristophanes* (Göttingen 1987), and "Some Deceptions in Aristophanes," in F. Cairns and M. Heath, eds., *Papers of the Leeds International Latin Seminar* 6 (1990):229–40; S. Goldhill, *The Poet's Voice* (London 1991):167–223; Halliwell (see note 6), and also "Comic satire and freedom of speech in classical Athens," *Journal of Hellenic Studies* 111 (1991):48–70; J. C. Carrière, *Le Carnaval et la Politique* (Paris 1979); F. Muecke, "A portrait of the artist as a young woman," *Classical Quarterly* 32 (1982):41–55; L. Taaffe, *Aristophanes and Women* (London 1993).

One of the most striking features of Old Comedy was personal humor, jokes against real people who were probably sitting in the audience at the time.[45] Later antiquity would fasten on *to onomasti komodein* ("to make fun of by name") as the quintessence of Old Comedy. The origins of comedy are explained by outlining how personal jokes came to be part of public festivals; the end of Old Comedy is explained by laws on personal humor or the rise of oligarchy ("fear fell on the poets"). Comedy thus acquired its redeeming social value, marking out those deserving of ridicule; for Horace (*Satires* I.4.1–7) comedy is the literary ancestor of his own satire:

> The poets Eupolis, Cratinus, and Aristophanes, indeed all the poets of Old Comedy, if there was any man deserving to be singled out as a bad man or a thief, because he was an adulterer, a pick-pocket or notorious in some way, they would attack them with great freedom.

It is interesting to speculate on the sequence in which the Alexandrian critics worked. Did they fasten on the best-known threesome of Old Comedy (Cratinus, Eupolis, Aristophanes) and from their works deduce a political and satirical essence for the genre? This is the usual assumption among critics, but the opposite is possible, that the critics, proceeding perhaps on the same lines as Aristotle, first defined Old Comedy as political satire and then sought a comic threesome whose comedy fit that model.

Again, care must be used in assessing such jokes. Because Aristophanes makes fun of someone, does that indicate personal animosity or just the recognition that here was good humor? Was anyone ever hurt by comedy? Comedy is usually blamed for the Athenian hostility against Socrates (see Plato *Apol.* 19c, *Phd.* 70b), but Plato is writing well after the fact and looking for someone to blame. Was there even a sense of having arrived if one was prominent enough to be the target of comedy? In other words, could Athenians take a joke? Cleon, it appears, could not, but Lucian's words (second century C.E.) in the mouth of Philosophy are intriguing:

> Is that all you're worried about? A few rude remarks? You know the way that Comedy treats me at the Dionysia, but we're still the best of

---

[45] Consult Halliwell (see note 6) and Storey (1998) here.

friends. I've never taken her to court or even complained privately to her. I just let her enjoy the fun that's all part and parcel of the festival. For I know that no harm can come from a joke. (*Halieus* 14)

In the case of the three great caricatures in Aristophanes (Euripides, Cleon, and Socrates), I see the first as essentially complimentary with the proviso that by the time of *Frogs*, Aristophanes recognized that Euripides' tragedy was wonderful but fundamentally subversive, the second as hostile with more than a little malice, and the last a joke that got away from its creator.

So what does one say in the end about Aristophanes? He is, I think, a traditionalist, a supporter of the "good old days," a democrat who would prefer leaders from the *kaloi k'agathoi* rather than these upstarts from the mercantile class—Aristophanes is something of a snob—but above all a poet who possesses the same qualities that he attributes to Euripides: *sophos* ("wise"), *dexios* ("clever"), and *gonimos* ("creative"). He excels at comedy of the imagination, the creation of wonderful fantasies, the development and execution of these ideas, and a great variety of humors. He can take us to Olympus on the back of a dung-beetle, into the war between the sexes with brilliant effect, to the Underworld in search of a poet "who can save our city." Aeschylus and Euripides duel for the throne of tragedy and for the salvation of Athens, and they agree that the criteria for good art are "technical skill and making the people better citizens" (*Frogs* 1009). Aristophanes, I think, is saying in *Frogs* that for a poet who combines both and whose theme is *ta dikaia* ("what is right"), you need look no further than the comedian you are watching.

Clouds

Clouds is certainly Aristophanes' best-known comedy. If modern readers know one of his plays, it is usually this one, although in the late years of the twentieth century, *Lysistrata* may run a close second. The manuscript tradition and the accompanying scholia are by far the fullest for *Clouds*, and the anecdotal tradition in ancient authors concerning this play is equally large.[46] This is of course due to the

---

[46]These are collected (in Greek) at K–A III.2 11–16.

presence of the august (dare one say "saintly"?) figure of Socrates in the comedy. Plato and Xenophon created a character of legendary importance in classical culture, and Aristophanes' contemporary caricature of him attracted a huge amount of attention.

The play revolves around an old country farmer, Strepsiades ("Twister"), whose son, Pheidippides, has run him deeply into debt through an upper-class lifestyle and a passion for horses. His "great idea": for his son to enter the *phrontisterion* ("Pondertorium") of Socrates where he will learn the Inferior Argument, which "can debate an unjust case and win" (115), and thus talk his way out of his father's debts. When the son refuses to obey, Strepsiades goes himself to learn from Socrates. The play proceeds in four movements: (a) 1–509, his introduction and initiation to the Pondertorium, and meeting with the chorus of Clouds, new deities who preside over the "new learning,"[47] (b) the parabasis (510–626), a choral digression, (c) a teaching scene (627–803) in which the old man fails miserably at learning and remembering anything at all, a brief scene (814–888) in which the son is dragooned into attending after all, and then quite a good agon (889–1113) between the Inferior and Superior Arguments— Pheidippides will study with the winner (who turns out to be the Inferior), and (d) the consequences of the "new learning" (1131–end), which do result in Strepsiades' avoiding his debts but with results that he could not have foreseen—the "new learning" will lead one to prefer Euripides over Aeschylus and to beat one's parents. In a strange *volte-face* the Clouds reveal themselves as agents of the traditional gods (1457-61), and after admitting the error of his ways, Strepsiades proceeds to burn down the Pondertorium.

Whitman argued that Aristophanic comedy featured a recurring type of comic hero, the old countryman who achieves his great idea and comes out on top through a streak of *poneria* ("knavery," "roguishness") at the heart of his personality, and Strepsiades certainly fits this model. Much is made in the prologue of his country roots and attitudes, as opposed to the luxury (decadence?) of the town, and while he may lack the grandiose imagination of Dicaeopolis (*Acharnians*) or Peithetaerus (*Birds*), the earnestness of Trygaeus (*Peace*) or Lysistrata, or the irrepressibility of Procleon

---

[47]On the chorus and its identity in the comedy see Segal, Dover (*Cl.*) lxv–lxx, and Bowie (1993) 124–30.

(*Wasps*), he does possess a down-to-earth cunning, a simplicity that the spectator will find appealing. Simply put, he is the ideal sort to "take the piss" out of sophistic pretensions. The teaching scene (627–804) shows Aristophanes at his comic best where the less-than-bright Strepsiades foils every attempt by Socrates to teach him anything. Yet the scene depends on stretching the spectator's reactions in two opposite directions: he wants to be a *sophos* like Socrates, for (unlike Strepsiades) he knows about measures and rhythms, and at the same time wants to see the *sophos* taken down a rung or two. We admire Strepsiades' low cunning and desire not to pay his debts, but at the same time we wince at his essential dishonesty and insistence at learning the Inferior Argument.[48] It can be observed that the "great idea" is undone at the end, that Strepsiades repents of what he has done (1462–4), that the play ends with destruction rather than jubilation or reconciliation. But the ending is one place that we know was altered in the revision, and the original may well have ended differently.

Clouds may be less "political" than other plays of the 420s—if it were not for the passing reference at line 7, we would not know that Athens was at war at this time—but it is no less topical. *Clouds* dramatizes a contact with what we call the "Enlightenment," the intellectual fervor that burst on the Greeks in the fifth century. Beginning with the Ionian physical scientists of the sixth century, it went far beyond inquiries on the physical nature of the universe; the thinkers of the fifth century raised the great questions of ethics, being, political science, anthropology, language, and even of the nature of knowledge itself.[49] These included the great philosophers such as Parmenides, Heraclitus, and Anaxagoras, but of more importance for this comedy were the sophists, the professional teachers who traveled from city to city claiming to teach knowledge and skills, including public oratory, making the weaker case appear the stronger (112–15). The most familiar are Protagoras ("man is a measure of all things"), Hippias, Prodicus (see line 361), and

---

[48]If a modern parallel be sought, we need look no further than Homer Simpson (*The Simpsons*), whose essential character trait must be *poneria* and who elicits both exasperation and sympathy from millions of viewers.

[49]The literature here is immense. I refer the interested student to W. K. C. Guthrie, *A History of Greek Philosophy*, vol. 2 and 3 (Cambridge 1965/1969), and to G. Kerferd, *The Sophistic Movement* (Cambridge 1981).

Gorgias; Plato's dialogues (especially *Protagoras* and *Gorgias*) present a somewhat unflattering picture of these men, who at times are portrayed as "con artists" or "snake-oil salesmen." And then there is Socrates, the only Athenian among these intellectuals, who was especially interested in knowledge and ethics, who was anything but a sophist, at least if Plato and Xenophon are to be trusted.[50] Physically distinctive (with a face like a satyr) and given to strange habits (walking barefoot with a distinctive gait, wearing light clothing, rolling his eyes), he was a comedian's godsend, and what Aristophanes has done is take this familiar Athenian, now in his 40s, who moved in important company, and turn him into an itinerant sophist.

At line 1399 Pheidippides speaks for so many of the "Enlightenment" when he exclaims, "How pleasurable it is to be acquainted with modern ways and intelligent notions." The wave of fresh thought, of questioning traditional views, of challenging the status quo must have been much like the spirit of change that flowed through the 1960s. The key word is "new," for we see new gods and deities (Clouds and Vortex), new words (943, 1397), new principles and techniques (480, 897), the new education (936), and even new laws (1423). *Clouds* deals with the encounter by the old and unsophisticated Strepsiades with the new world of thoughts and thinkers. There is one other reference to newness, or innovation, in this play, at line 547, but this is the innovation of Aristophanes, part of his new and clever comedy—at *Wasps* 1044 referring to *Clouds* he "sowed a crop of new concepts"—and this should give us pause before we assume that for Aristophanes "old" was good and "new" bad. "Clever," "new," and "wise" are words that apply to the "new learning" and also to Aristophanes' own comedy.[51]

The principal problem in dealing with *Clouds* is the portrait of Socrates and what this says about Aristophanes' personal and comic intentions. The Socrates in the comedy and the Socrates that we know from Plato and Xenophon are simply not the same. The comic

---

[50]Socrates left no written works, and we depend on the portraits drawn by Plato in his dialogues, who did not begin to write until after Socrates' death in 399, and by Xenophon in his *Memoirs*, also later than 399. One well-known saying sums up Socrates' ethical belief, "no-one does wrong knowingly."

[51]See Cartledge 22–31 and Bowie (1993) 132.

Socrates teaches in a school, charges fees for instruction, gives lessons in the physical sciences, grammar, music, and rhetoric, and disbelieves in the traditional gods, all of which are expressly denied in various places in the works of Plato and Xenophon. The comic portrait agrees with the real Socrates on physical details only (his gait, bare feet, rolling eyes, etc.). After an exhaustive examination of the evidence, Dover concludes that "Plato and Xenophon tell the truth: Ar. attaches to Socrates the characteristics which belonged to the sophists in general but did not belong to Socrates" (xlix). Socrates was an attractive target—he was Athenian and physically distinctive, the perfect focus for a comedy about ideas and intellectuals.

This leads to the larger question—what was Aristophanes' purpose in this? A number of approaches have been followed, which can be summarized briefly as (a) hostility and malice, (b) pure comedy with more than a hint of appreciation for Socrates, and (c) an "us against them" mentality. The first approach has commended itself to those who see Aristophanes as a traditionalist who hated anything new (demagogues, Euripides, intellectuals), as a man who saw new ideas, in art or in science, as essentially dangerous. The main problem here is that the old men in the play, Strepsiades and Superior Argument, are hardly paragons of virtue or intellect; and if the new is being compared unfavorably to the old, then the old fails to live up to any standard.[52] There is much to be said for (b), most eloquently stated by Murray. I have mentioned that both Socrates and Aristophanes have newness, wisdom, and cleverness in common, and the sympathetic picture of Aristophanes in Plato's *Symposium* reveals a comedian with affinities to the Socratic circle. At one point (221b) Alcibiades even refers to the picture of Socrates in *Clouds* with no hint of rancor. Some have objected that this requires a cynical disregard on Aristophanes' part, that he would knowingly caricature falsely a man known to him,

---

[52]Norwood 219 ff. saw the Superior Argument as essentially attractive and positive, but Dover (*Cl.*) lxiv provides a useful corrective, "apart from the inability to meet reasonable argument with anything better than an outburst of bad temper . . . the most striking characteristic of Right ["Superior Argument"] is his obsession with boys' genitals." Both Arguments have their moments, and good comedy will allow the spectator to sympathize with and laugh at both.

but Aristophanes' skill is precisely that, willful distortion and exaggeration. A passage in Plutarch records Socrates' alleged reaction to *Clouds*, "I feel that I am being made fun of by friends at a great party" (Plutarch *Moralia* 10c–d). This may be how the joke was intended and taken.

I have less sympathy with (c). It argues for an Aristophanes who really did not understand the difference between Socrates and a sophist, or if he did, that it did not concern him a great deal.[53] On this view Aristophanes is the spokesman for "us" against "them," where "them" includes poets, philosophers, politicians, etc. Socrates is a representative of the abnormal and thus good comic material; whether the caricature is fair or not is not really the point. My problem here is that Aristophanes is hardly the "average man," but rather a superior poet who saw himself as the brilliant teacher and savior of the city. He is really one of "them," one of the *sophoi*, not one of *hoi polloi*. He belongs with Euripides and Socrates, not against them. We must assume, I think, that he knew the difference between Socrates and a sophist, and that as a comedian he could not pass up the opportunity that Socrates provided. He was the obvious target for a caricature of the intellectual movement.

The play itself was produced at the Dionysia of 423, and gained the third prize—the winner being Cratinus with *Pytine* ("Wine Flask") and second place going to Ameipsias' *Connus*.[54] But the text we have is not that of the original production; this becomes abundantly clear at 518 ff., when the chorus talks of the previous failure of "this comedy" and at 553 mentions Eupolis' *Maricas*, which was not produced until 421, at the Lenaea. This part of the parabasis certainly belongs to a revision. The actual details of the lost first *Clouds* and the implications for production will be considered in the appendix, but it is clear that what we have is a partial and not completed revision that was never produced on stage. Thus, the student should use care in treating this text as an organic whole, which it is not, and refrain from drawing conclusions

---

[53]See Dover (*Cl.*) xxxii–lvii and J. Henderson in Sommerstein et al. (1993) 307–19.

[54]*Pytine* was a brilliant piece of metatheatre, which I have discussed earlier in the Introduction. Ameipsias' play seems to have focused on a musician (Connus) and had a chorus of *phrontistai* ("thinkers").

about Aristophanes' technique and attitudes, since we do not know either what was in the original or what the completed revision would have looked like. The critical judgment that one brings to *Birds* or *Wasps* or *Frogs* should be suspended here.

Ian C. Storey

Diagram of the Stage

Hypothetical reconstruction of the Theatre of Dionysus, c.458 B.C.E. (according to Meineck). In the orchestra are uncostumed blocking mannequins, as seen from approximately ten tiers above the first seating row (seating not shown). Scholars are divided both on whether there was a raised stage at this period, and, if so, its height.

Translator's Preface

This translation of *Clouds*, like the translations of *Wasps* and *Birds* with which it was first published,* began its creative life as a play text for performance, and is a result of eight years of work on ancient comedy with the Aquila Theatre Company and before that, the London Small Theatre Company. I have had the pleasure of staging these translations in the United Kingdom, Canada, the United States, Holland, and Greece in a variety of theatres—from intimate black boxes, to large performing arts centers, to the ancient stadium at Delphi. In *Clouds*, as in the others, my aim has been to create a text that serves both as a tool for the effective execution of onstage comedy and as an accurate reflection of the Greek. I have benefited enormously from the work of scholars and translators such as Alan Sommerstein, Sir Kenneth Dover, Douglass Parker, William Arrowsmith, and others who have contributed to our understanding of the genius of Aristophanic comedy, and I have based my translation of *Clouds* primarily on the Greek text edited by Sommerstein (*Clouds* 1982).

That sound scholarship is essential to any translation of an ancient play goes without saying, but what about the lessons learned from performance? A play is only created for performance, and its

---

Aristophanes 1: Clouds, Wasps, Birds, translated, with notes, by Peter Meineck; introduced by Ian C. Storey (Indianapolis: Hackett Publishing Company, 1998).

existence as a written text is subordinate to its primary form and function as a live, shared experience between actors and audience. But can a contemporary, English-language production of an Aristophanes play, any more than a script that gives directions for one, still be called an experience of Aristophanes? True, there are as many differences between contemporary theatre and that of late fifth century B.C.E., as there are similarities, but the essential aim of Aristophanes to provoke, poke fun at, celebrate, analyze, and criticize the society around him can still manifest itself as a potent dramatic force today: fathers and sons still battle across the generation gap, legal systems are still perceived as ineffective, politicians are still accused of corruption, new ideas and intellectual movements still provoke laughter and cause misunderstandings. People are still in debt, still trying to escape the hustle and bustle of everyday life, still looking for their own Cloudcuckoolands.

I have chosen not to update the contemporary references in these translations. A joke about a politician's errant behavior in the news today will seem as out of date to an audience or reader in five years as will a reference to Cleon or Alcibiades. It never ceases to amaze me how the combined creativity of a well informed director and actor can take what seem to be obscure and inappropriate ancient references and communicate them directly and immediately on stage, with a facial expression, a movement, or the manipulation of body language. An understanding of the times in which the plays were produced is essential to this approach. With this in mind, I have employed two types of notes to help the reader gain a better understanding of these plays. The footnotes on the page are intended quickly to inform while not distracting from the flow of the play, while the endnotes provide more detailed discussion of certain subjects and point to ancient evidence and supporting scholarship. These notes may also help provide insight into some of my translation choices. In the instances where I have adapted a phrase or reference into a contemporary form to keep its sense or humor, I have included a closer translation of the Greek in the notes.

Theatre is, of course, a Greek word that means "Seeing Place"; thus I have tried to bring a visual dimension to these translations with detailed stage directions and references in the endnotes to pictorial evidence for many of the stage properties and costumes found in the plays. Aristophanes gets enormous comic mileage out of common household utensils and everyday objects, and it is important to provide the interested reader with information as to where representations can be found. I have attempted to keep the number of supporting works to a minimum, drawing most examples from John Boardman's Thames and Hudson series on Greek vase painting and sculpture.

The Greek texts have come down to us without stage directions, and sometimes we cannot say for certain which line should be assigned to which character. Some sense of the structure of the play can be gleaned from textual indications, and I have made decisions on entrances and exits based on my own sense of dramatic structure and knowledge of the physical staging conditions of the Greek theatre. Although I have had the opportunity to work extensively with masks and stage live performances at both Epidaurus and Delphi (as well as in hundreds of modern stages), it is impossible to know for certain the exact stage movements of these plays.

My overall aim has been to produce a translation that is understandable, performable, accessible, and entertaining. I have not attempted to replicate the meter of the Greek, but I have adopted the same basic line divisions to assist text referencing. One of the most satisfying parts of my work has been to hear an audience in Athens, Georgia, still laughing at the same joke 2500 years after it was first delivered in Athens, Greece. Aristophanes is undoubtedly one of the world's greatest comic dramatists; his work offers us a direct connection with our past, and I hope this volume will in some small way help further our understanding and appreciation of this daring, provocative, and hilarious genius.

Peter Meineck

Clouds

Strepsiades (center) and characters from *Clouds*. The London
Small Theatre Company, Amsterdam 1990

Cast of Characters

STREPSIADES	a rural Athenian
PHEIDIPPIDES	son of Strepsiades
HOUSEBOY	of Strepsiades
STUDENTS	of Socrates
SOCRATES	a philosopher
CHORUS	of Clouds
SUPERIOR ARGUMENT	
INFERIOR ARGUMENT	
FIRST CREDITOR	
SECOND CREDITOR	
CHAEREPHON	a philosopher
XANTHIAS	servant to Strepsiades

Clouds was first produced by Aristophanes in 423 B.C.E., at the Dionysia Festival in the city of Athens. This translation was inspired by a production by the London Small Theatre Company, which received its first U.K. public performance at the Shaw Theatre, London, in January 1990 and its first U.S. public performance at the Judith Anderson Theatre, New York, in May 1990, directed by Fiona Laird and produced by Peter Meineck.

* refers to an endnote (found at the end of the play).
Each footnote is preceded by the line number to which it refers.

Clouds

SCENE: *A house in Athens.*

(An old man named Strepsiades and his son Pheidippides are asleep. Strepsiades is tossing and turning and muttering to himself until he finally wakes up with a start.)*

STREPSIADES:
  Oh! Oh!
  Oh, Zeus almighty! What a night!
  It's never-ending! It must be morning soon.
  I thought I heard the cock crow hours ago.
  Just listen to those blasted servants, snoring away,   5
  back in my day they'd have never dared to sleep in.
  Damn this stupid war! It'll ruin us. I can't even beat my own
      slaves anymore
  in case they sneak off and hide out in enemy territory!*

  (Pointing to Pheidippides)

  Just look at him, the "refined young gentleman," he'll never see
      the sunrise,
  he'll just carry on, blissfully farting away under his five fluffy
      blankets.   10

8: For more than seven years Athens and Sparta had been engaged in the
Peloponnesian War.

3

It's all right for some! Oh, I'll just try and bury my head and
ignore the snoring.

*(Strepsiades tries to go back to sleep, he tosses and turns and then
angrily throws off the covers in frustration.)*

It's no good, I just can't sleep!
I'm being bitten by debts and eaten away by stable bills.
Why? Because of this long-haired son of mine,
15   and all his riding events and chariot races.
He lives, breathes, and dreams horses!
It's already the 20th day of the month,
and the interest is due on the 30th. I'm finished!

(He calls out to a slave.)

Boy! Light a lamp and fetch my ledger!
20   I need to count up my debts and calculate the interest.

*(A slave hurries from the stage right door with some tablets and a
lamp. He hands the tablets to Strepsiades and holds the lamp so he
can read the accounts.)*

Now then, let's have a look at these debts:
"Twelve hundred drachmas owed to Pasias." Twelve hundred
drachmas!
What on earth was that for? Oh, gods, I remember now, a horse
for Pheidippides!
Twelve hundred drachmas? Ouch! I think I was the one taken for
a ride.*

(Pheidippides, dreaming of chariot races, mutters in his sleep.)

PHEIDIPPIDES:
25   Philon, you cheat, keep to your own lane!

STREPSIADES:
You hear that! That's the problem right there.
He's constantly at the races, even in his sleep!

14: Long hair was considered a Spartan fashion and was worn by aspiring
young aristocrats with antidemocratic sentiments (see *Wasps* line 476).

PHEIDIPPIDES:
How many turns must the war chariots make?

STREPSIADES:
Enough to turn your father into a pauper!
"What terrible debt shall strike after Pasias' bills?   30
Three hundred drachmas owed to Amynias
for a running board and a new set of wheels!"

PHEIDIPPIDES:
Make sure my horse has a roll before he goes home!

STREPSIADES:
It's my money those damned horses are rolling in!
While I am saddled with lawsuits and debts
and my creditors can't wait to seize my property.   35

    (Pheidippides wakes up.)

PHEIDIPPIDES:
What is it, father? Is it really necessary to spend
the entire night twisting and writhing about?

STREPSIADES:
I'm being bitten to death . . . by bed bailiffs!*

PHEIDIPPIDES:
Please, father. I am trying to get some sleep!

    (Pheidippides settles down back to sleep.)

STREPSIADES:
Go on then, sleep away, soon enough all this will be yours.   40
My debts will be on your head one day! Sleep away, my boy.
Oh, I wish I had never met your mother, and I hope whoever it was

---

31: Amynias was lampooned in comedy as an upper-class, long-haired
good for nothing (see *Wasps* line 74).

32: These lines are adapted from a lost Euripides play (fr. 1011), "What
terrible thing will strike the house?"

who introduced us dies a horribly cruel death!
Ah yes, those were the days, a lovely country life,
full of simple rustic pleasures. An unwashed, unshaven heaven,
45   abounding with honey bees, shaggy sheep, lashings of olive oil . . .
then I married the niece of Megacles, son of Megacles.
I was just a plain country boy, but she was from the city
and had all these refined and delicate ways. A proper little lady.*
And when we were joined together as man and wife, I went to bed
50   smelling fresh and fruity, like ripe figs and new wool.
She smelled of fine perfume, golden saffron, sexy kisses,
extravagance and luxury. Aphrodite all over and everywhere Eros.*
Mind you, I can't say that she's lazy, not at all, she knew how to
      weave,
If you know what I mean. In-out, in-out, she loved to poke the
      thread!
It got to the point that I had to hold up my gown, show the
      evidence,
and tell her that it would wear out if she kept on whacking it like
55   that!*

(Strepsiades lifts his gown to reveal a limp phallus.)

HOUSEBOY:
There's no oil left in the lamp.

STREPSIADES:
Why did you use the thirstiest lamp in the house?
You've earned a beating. Come here.

HOUSEBOY:
                                        Why should I?

46: Megacles was a common name of the prominent aristocratic
Alcmaeonid clan. Both Pericles and Alcibiades were related.

51: Saffron was the traditional golden yellow color of female festive robes
and a bride's wedding veil.

56: A reference to Strepsiades' lack of sexual prowess in old age.

STREPSIADES:
Because you inserted a thick wick, that's why!

(The houseboy exits through the stage right door.)

Where was I? Oh yes. Well, soon enough we had a son,   *60*
and then my troubles really began. The wife and I could not agree
on a name for the boy. She wanted something upper-class and
   horsey,
a name with *hippus* in it, like "Xanthippus," "Chaerippus," or
   "Callippides."
But I wanted to name him Pheidonides after his grandfather,
   a good old-fashioned thrifty name.
We argued for ages, then eventually we reached a compromise   *65*
and gave him the name Pheidippides.
When he was little she used to take him in her arms and say,
"When you grow up, you'll be a rich man like uncle Megacles
and drive a chariot through the city wearing a beautiful golden
   robe."*   *70*
But I would tell him, "When you're big you'll be just like your
   father
and drive goats down from the mountains, wearing a lovely
   leather jerkin."
But he never listened to a single word I said,
it was like flogging a dead horse, and now the household
   accounts
have a severe case of "galloping consumption."   *75*
I've been up all night trying to concoct a plan to get me out of this
   mess,
and I have found one drastic course, an extraordinary, supernatural
   trail.
If I can only persuade the lad to take it, I'll be saved!

63: Names containing *hippus* ("horse") were popular with the Athenian
upper classes. Aristophanes' father was named Phillippus.

64: Pheidonides means "son of thrifty."

66: The name means something like "Spare the horses."

70: A victory in the Panathenaic games won the charioteer the right of
riding in the procession to the Acropolis wearing a golden cloak (*70 **Drive
a chariot**).

Now then, let me think what would be the gentlest way to wake
him up . . .?

(Strepsiades leans over and whispers in Pheidippides' ear.)

80   Pheidipoo, little Pheidipoo . . .

*(There is no response from Pheidippides, Strepsiades becomes
frustrated and shouts.)*

PHEIDIPPIDES!

(Pheidippides wakes with a start.)

PHEIDIPPIDES:
What! What do you want, father?

STREPSIADES:
Give me a kiss and take my hand.

(He does so.)

PHEIDIPPIDES:
All right. What is it?

STREPSIADES:
Tell me, son, do you love me?

PHEIDIPPIDES:
By Poseidon, god of horses, of course I do!

STREPSIADES:
I don't want to hear about the god of horses!
85   He's the very reason that I'm in this mess.
Listen, son, if you really love me, will you do what I ask?

PHEIDIPPIDES:
What would you like me to do?

83: Poseidon was the second patron deity of Athens after Athena, god of
the sea, "Earthshaker," and father of horses (***83 God of horses**).

STREPSIADES:
 Turn your life around, right now,
 do what I say, and go and learn.

PHEIDIPPIDES:
 Learn what? 90

STREPSIADES:
 Will you do it?

PHEIDIPPIDES:
 (Exasperated) I'll do it, by Dionysus!

STREPSIADES:
 Great! Now look over there *(he points to the stage left door)*.
 Can you see that tiny doorway and that funny little house?

PHEIDIPPIDES:
 I see it, what are you showing me, father?

STREPSIADES:
 That, my boy, is the house of clever souls, the Pondertorium. 95
 The men who live there are able to talk us into believing
 that the universe is a casserole dish that covers us all
 and we are the hot coals, nestling inside.*
 What's more, for a small fee, these gentleman they will teach you
 how to successfully argue any case, right or wrong.

PHEIDIPPIDES:
 Who are these people? 100

STREPSIADES:
 I'm not sure I know their names, but they are all gentlemen,
 good and true, and fine philosophers of the finite.

PHEIDIPPIDES:
 Ughh! I know who you mean, that godforsaken bunch

91: Dionysus was the god of wine, revelry, and the theatre.

of pasty looking frauds, going around barefoot!*
You're talking about Socrates and Chaerephon!

STREPSIADES:

105   Shut up! Stop talking like a baby.
Consider your father's daily bread, there'll be none left,
unless you give up horse racing and sign up for classes.

PHEIDIPPIDES:

No, by Dionysus, no! Not even if you gave me
a pair of Leogoras' finest pheasants!

STREPSIADES:

110   Please! My darling little boy, I beg you. Go and be taught.

PHEIDIPPIDES:

But what do I need to learn?

STREPSIADES:

I have heard it said, that in this house reside two different
kinds of argument, one is called the Superior Argument,
whatever that is, and the other is known as the Inferior Argument.*
115   Some men say that the Inferior Argument can debate an unjust case
and win. All you have to do is learn this Inferior Argument for me,
then you can talk your way out of all the debts I've incurred
on your behalf, and I won't have to repay a single obol!

PHEIDIPPIDES:

No, I won't do it! How could I bear to show my pallid face
to all my friends in the cavalry? Wild horses couldn't drag me in
120   there!

104: A philosopher-colleague of Socrates (*104 Chaerephon).

109: Leogoras came from an old, established Athenian family and was known for his expensive tastes (see *Wasps* line 1269). Pheasants were a rare species in Greece and an expensive luxury.

118: An obol was a small Athenian coin. Six obols were equal to one drachma.

120: The Athenian cavalry (*hippeis*) was an exclusive corps of around a thousand wealthy young upper-class citizens who could afford the expense of a horse and armor.

STREPSIADES:

Then get out of my house, by Demeter! You'll not get another crumb
out of me. And that goes for your chariot stallion and your branded
thoroughbred. I've had enough of your horsing around!

PHEIDIPPIDES:

I'll just go to uncle Megacles. He'll make sure
that I'm not without horse and home!   125

> *(Exit Pheidippides through the stage right door.)*

STREPSIADES:

I'm not down and out yet! With the help of the gods,
I'll enroll at the Pondertorium and learn it all myself!

> *(Strepsiades strides off toward the stage left door, then slows down
> and stops.)*

Oh, I'm just a stupid old fool. How on earth can I be expected
to learn all those hair-splitting arguments at my age?
I'm far too old, and my mind's certainly not what it used to be.   130

> *(He turns around and sets off for the stage right door, then
> suddenly stops.)*

No! I have to do it! It's my one and only chance.
No more delaying, I'm going to walk right up and knock on the door!

> *(He marches purposefully up to the stage left door, knocks hard,
> and shouts out.)*

Boy! Boy! Where are you? Boy!

> *(The stage left door-hatch opens suddenly.)*

STUDENT:

Go to Hell!

> *(The student slams the hatch shut. Strepsiades knocks on the door
> again, and the hatch reopens.)*

Who's there?

121: Demeter was the goddess of the harvest.

STREPSIADES:
Strepsiades, son of Pheidon, from Cicynna.

STUDENT:
Obviously an uneducated idiot! Don't you realize that you
135   thoughtlessly
banged away at the door with such force that you may well have
    caused
the miscarriage of a brilliant new idea on the verge of discovery!

STREPSIADES:
I'm very sorry, I'm from far away, in the country.
What was it that may have "miscarried"?

(The student furtively looks around, then leans in to whisper.)

STUDENT:
140 Only students may be told such things. It is the sacred law.

(Strepsiades mimics the student's movements and also whispers.)

STREPSIADES:
It's quite all right, you can tell me,
I've come to sign up as a student at the Pondertorium.

(The stage left door opens, and the student breaks into normal speech.)

STUDENT:
Very well, but remember these things are holy mysteries and must
be kept secret. Just now, Socrates asked Chaerephon how many
feet a flea could jump, calculating the equation of one flea foot for
145   a foot.
This question came to Chaerephon's mind, as the flea in question
had just bitten his eyebrow and leapt onto Socrates' head.*

134: The exact location of Cicynna is not known, but it was probably a rural Attic *deme* (district).

143: Secret initiation rites such as those at Eleusis that promised life after death were called "The Mysteries."

STREPSIADES:
How did he measure the distance?

STUDENT:
Expertly. He dipped the flea's feet in some melted wax,
and when it had dried, he carefully removed the molds,   150
producing a pair of Persian booties in miniature.
He was halfway through measuring the distance when you . . .

STREPSIADES:
Zeus almighty! What a delicate, subtle intellect!

STUDENT:
You should have heard the new concept that Socrates recently
announced.

STREPSIADES:
What concept? Tell me, I beg you!   155

STUDENT:
Chaerephon of Sphettus asked Socrates to pronounce
his opinion on an important scientific matter.

STREPSIADES:
What was that?

STUDENT:
Whether the hum of a gnat is generated via its mouth or its anus.

STREPSIADES:
Really? And what did he find out about the gnat?

STUDENT:
He said that the intestine of a gnat is extremely constricted   160
and that air is pressed through this narrow conduit to the anus,
then the sphincter, acting as an oscillating cavity in close proximity

---

151: These were soft calf-length leather boots (*151 **Booties**).

156: Sphettus was an Attic deme. Aristophanes may be continuing the
insect gags with a pun based on *sphex* ("wasp").

to a compressed channel, is forced to issue a vibrating sound
as a direct result of the wind acting upon it.

STREPSIADES:
165   So a gnat's arse is a trumpet! Who'd have thought it?
What an amazing display of rectumology; really gutsy stuff!
I'm sure Socrates could easily fend off hostile legal actions
with such a deep understanding of arseholes.

STUDENT:
Yesterday he was robbed of a stupendous new idea by a speckled
gecko.

STREPSIADES:
170   What? Tell me more.

STUDENT:
He was preoccupied studying the lunar revolutions,
and as he stood there gaping at the night sky,
a speckled gecko on the roof shat right on his head.

STREPSIADES:
(Laughing) A speckled gecko shitting on Socrates, I like that.

STUDENT:
175   Then, last evening there was nothing for supper.

STREPSIADES:
Really? So how did he think he was going to get some oats?

STUDENT:
First, he laid the table by sprinkling a thin layer of ash over it,
then he bowed a skewer to form a pair of compasses, picked up
the bent legs . . . from the wrestling school and stole his cloak!

174: The Turkish gecko has a spotted skin that resembles stars; hence its
Latin name *Stellio* (*174 **Speckled gecko**).

179: This joke hinges on the word *diabêtês*, which can mean both a pair of
compasses or "bestrider." The wrestling schools were popular places for
meeting young men, and Socrates often taught there. Both Plato's "Academy"
and Aristotle's "Lyceum" were wrestling schools (*179 **Wrestling school**).

Strepsiades:

Amazing! And to think, some people still think highly of Thales! *180*
Come on, open, open the Pondertorium!
Quickly, I want to see *him*. I want to meet Socrates!
I can't wait any longer, I'm dying to learn. Open the door!

> *(The central doors open and the ekkyklema is rolled out onstage. A group of four pallid, barefooted and shabbily dressed students are revealed busy with various activities.)*

By Heracles! What on earth are these creatures!

Student:

You seem surprised. What do you think they are? *185*

Strepsiades:

They look like a bunch of half-starved walking wounded to me.*

> *(Pointing to a group of the students)*

Why are they staring at the ground?

Student:

They are seeking to know what lies beneath the earth.

Strepsiades:

I see, they're looking for onions to eat. They don't need to waste time
pondering about that, I know just where they can find some lovely
   big ones.
(Pointing to another group) Why are they bending over like that? *190*

Student:

They are probing the nether regions of Erebus deep beneath Tartarus.

180: Thales (c.625–c.545) was one of the "Seven Sages" and was regarded as
the father of natural philosophy.

188: The study of subterranean phenomena was considered heretical by
many Athenians as an affront to the realm of Hades (**188 What lies
beneath**).

192: Erebus and Tartarus were the darkest and bleakest regions of the
Underworld (see *Birds* line 661).

STREPSIADES:
Really? So why are their arses pointing at the sky?

STUDENT:
They are simultaneously studying "arse-stronomy!"
195   *(To the students)* Back inside! He must not find you out here.

STREPSIADES:
Hold on! Not so fast. Let them stay awhile,
I'd like to probe them with a penetrating point.

> *(Exit the students on the ekkyklema, which moves back behind the doors.)*

STUDENT:
Sorry. It's against all the rules. It's not good for them
to spend too much time outside, exposed to the fresh air.

> *(Strepsiades notices a strange array of ludicrous scientific instruments.)*

STREPSIADES:
200   What, in the name of the gods, might these be?

STUDENT:
This is for astronomy.*

STREPSIADES:
What's this for?

STUDENT:
Geometry.

STREPSIADES:
Geometry? What's that?

STUDENT:
It is the science of measuring the land.

STREPSIADES:
I see, to measure out plots for the landlords?*

STUDENT:
No, to measure land generally.

STREPSIADES:
Lovely! What a very democratic mechanism. 205

(The student shows Strepsiades a large map.)

STUDENT:
This is a map of the entire world. Look, here is Athens.

STREPSIADES:
Don't be stupid, that can't be Athens!
Where are all the jurors and the law courts?

STUDENT:
I'm telling you, this area is clearly the region of Attica.

STREPSIADES:
So where's my deme then? Where's Cicynna? 210

STUDENT:
I don't know! Over there somewhere. You see here, that is Euboea,
the long island lying off the coast.

STREPSIADES:
Yeah, me and Pericles really laid those revolting bastards out!
Where's Sparta then?

STUDENT:
Right here.

STREPSIADES:
That's far too close! You need to move it immediately! 215
You had better reponder that one, mate!

213: Euboea, which lay off the cost of Boeotia, rebelled against Athenian
control in 446. It was reconquered by Pericles, who divided up much of the
land and awarded it to Athenian citizens.

STUDENT:
But it's simply not possible just to . . .

STREPSIADES:
Then you'll get a beating, by Zeus . . .

> (*Enter Socrates suspended over the stage on a rack by the stage crane.*)*

Who on earth is that man hanging about up there?

STUDENT:
Himself.

STREPSIADES:
Who's "Himself"?

STUDENT:
Socrates.

STREPSIADES:
220   Socrates! Call him over for me, will you?

STUDENT:
You call him! I'm, eh . . . very busy.

> (*Exit the student scurrying off through the stage left door.*)

STREPSIADES:
Socrates! Oh Socrates!

SOCRATES:
Why do you call me, ephemeral creature?*

STREPSIADES:
Socrates! What are you doing up there?

SOCRATES:
225   I walk the air in order to look down on the sun.

225: The Greek *periphronô* can mean "contemplate" or "hold in contempt"
(***225 Look down on the sun**).

STREPSIADES:
But why do you need to float on a rack to scorn the gods?
If you have to do it, why not do it on the ground?

SOCRATES:
In order that I may make exact discoveries of the highest nature!
Thus, my mind is suspended to create only elevated notions.
The grains of these thoughts then merge with the similar   230
atmosphere of thin air! If I had remained earthbound
and attempted to scrutinize the heights, I would have found
nothing; for the earth forces the creative juices to be drawn
to its core, depriving one of the all important "water on the brain!"

STREPSIADES:
Eh?   235
You mean, you need a good brainwashing to think such thoughts?*
Oh my dear Socrates, you must come down at once.
You must teach me all the things that I have come to learn.

    (*Socrates is lowered to the ground.*)

SOCRATES:
And just why have you come?

STREPSIADES:
I want to learn to debate.
I'm being besieged by creditors, all my worldly goods   240
are under threat of seizure, the bailiffs are banging on my door!

SOCRATES:
Did you fail to realize you were amassing such enormous debts?

STREPSIADES:
Oh, I tried to keep things on a tight rein, but it was like closing
the stable door after the horse had bolted. I want you to teach me

---

234: A parody of one of the main theories of the philosopher Diogenes of
Apollonia, who believed that intellectual ability was influenced by moisture
in the air. The dryer the air, the purer the thoughts. Because the earth held
moisture, the nearer the ground a creature lived, the less intelligent it would
be.

that other Argument of yours, the one that never pays its dues.
245   Name your price, whatever it takes, I swear by the gods to pay you!*

SOCRATES:
  (Laughing) "Swear by the gods"? We don't give credit to the gods
  here.

STREPSIADES:
  Then how do you make oaths? This all sounds very Byzantine to
  me.*

SOCRATES:
250   Do you really want to know the truth regarding matters of religion?

STREPSIADES:
  I do, by Zeus! Is that possible?

SOCRATES:
  And do you wish communion with the Clouds, to actually speak
  to our divinities?

STREPSIADES:
  Oh, yes please!

SOCRATES:
  Then lie down on this sacred couch.

STREPSIADES:
255   *(He does so.)* I'm lying down.

SOCRATES:
  Here, take this ritual wreath.

      (Socrates hands him a shabby-looking wreath.)

247: The Greek *nomisma* has the sense of both "belief" and "currency."

254: Being ceremonially seated or "enthronement" was part of the initiation
rites of the Corybantes and the Eleusinian Mysteries.

256: Wreaths were worn at many religious occasions, including initiation
rites and sacrificial ceremonies.

STREPSIADES:

A wreath? Gods no! Socrates, I don't want to be sacrificed!
You're not going to make a meal out of me!*

SOCRATES:

Don't worry, it's just a part of the initiation rites, everyone has to
do it.

STREPSIADES:

What do I get out of it?

SOCRATES:

Why, you will become a polished public speaker, a rattling castanet,*   260
the "flour" of finest orators. Now hold still . . .

(*Socrates sprinkles flour over Strepsiades.*)

STREPSIADES:

By Zeus, I'm no powder puff! I know when I'm getting a good
dusting!*

SOCRATES:

Silence! Speak no ill words, old man, and heed my invocation.
O master, our lord, infinite Air, upholder of the buoyant earth.
O radiant Ether, O reverend thunder-cracking Clouds, ascend!   265
Reveal yourselves, sacred ladies, emerge for those with higher
thoughts!

STREPSIADES:

Wait, wait! I need to wrap myself up first so I don't get soaked.
Dammit! I knew I shouldn't have left home without a hat.

SOCRATES:

Come, you illustrious Clouds, come and reveal yourselves to this
mortal.
From the sacred snow-capped crests of Olympus, from the festive
spiraling   270

264: The philosopher Diogenes believed that the earth was kept in position
by a surrounding cushion or a pedestal of air.

dances of the Sea-Nymphs in the lush gardens of the Ocean father;
from the shimmering waters of the Nile where you dip your
  golden goblets;
from lake Maeotis or the icy heights of Mount Mimas. Hear my
  prayer!
Receive our sacrifice and bless our sacred rites.

  (The Clouds are heard offstage.)

CHORUS:
 Arise, appear, ever-soaring Clouds,
275 *The shape of shimmering drops assume.*
 From mountain slopes, where forests crowd,
280 *From ocean depths where breakers boom.*

 Look down upon the vales and hills,
 See sacred earth where showers splash.
 The holy rivers where rainfall spills,
285 *The roaring sea's rush and dash.*

 Shake off the rain and misty haze,
 A shining radiance warms the sky.
 Upon this earth the Clouds will gaze
290 *Under the tireless gleam of heaven's eye.*

SOCRATES:
 Oh, magnificent, revered Clouds, you heard my summons. You
 came!
 Did you hear that sound? Those bellowing godlike thunderclaps?*

STREPSIADES:
 I revere you too, oh illustrious Clouds! Let me answer your
 rumbling part

271: Poseidon's garden of the Hesperides was said to lie on the western
shore of the ocean beyond the pillars of Heracles.

273: Lake Maeotis was the Greek name for the sea of Azov to the north of
the Black Sea in the Crimea. Mt. Mimas was the name for a a mountain in
Ionia (the west coast of modern day Turkey) that stood opposite the island
of Chios.

with a rumbling fart! You've put the wind up me all right, I'm all
　　a jitter!
I don't know if it's right or wrong, but I need to take a thundering
　　crap! 295

SOCRATES:

Will you stop messing about and behaving like one of those
　　wretched comic playwrights!
Speak no ill words, a mighty flurry of goddesses is on the move,
　　singing as they go.

　　(The chorus begins to enter the orchestra from left and right.
　　Strepsiades still cannot see them.)

CHORUS:

On to Athens, maidens bearing rain,
The hallowed land of Cecrops' race, 300
Where the initiates seek to attain
Acceptance to a sacred place.

The house of Mysteries for holy rites 305
And massive temples with statues grand.
The godly processions to sacred sites,
The splendid sacrifices that crown the land.

Celebrations held throughout the year 310
Then sweet Dionysus comes in spring.
And the resonant tone of the pipes we hear
As the joyous chorus dance and sing.

STREPSIADES:

Zeus! Socrates, you must tell me, who are these ladies singing
this amazing song? Are they some new breed of female idols? 315

300: Cecrops was the mythical original king of Athens and was born from
the earth of Attica (***300 Cecrops**).

305: This is the Attic cult sanctuary to Demeter and Persephone at Eleusis,
where the initiations into the Mysteries were held.

SOCRATES:
No, no, no. They are the heavenly Clouds, magnificent goddesses for men
of leisure. They grace us with our intellect, argumentative skills, perception,
hyperbolization, circumlocution, pulverization, and predomination!

STREPSIADES:
That's why my spirit has soared at the sound of their voices!
320   I'm raring to split hairs, quibble over windy intricacies, set notion against notion, and strike down arguments within counter-arguments!
Oh, Socrates, I can't wait any longer, I've just got to see them!

SOCRATES:
Then look over here, up at Mount Parnes. Here they come, delicately wafting down.

STREPSIADES:
Where? Where? I can't see! Show me.

SOCRATES:
There, there. Can you see them all? Floating down over hill and dale,
325   Look, there wafting toward us, to the left and right.*

STREPSIADES:
What on earth are you talking about! I can't see anything!

SOCRATES:
Look there, in the wings!

STREPSIADES:
Yes, I think I . . . I can just about make something out.

SOCRATES:
Are you completely blind! Surely you can see them now?

(The chorus is now assembled in the orchestra.)

323: The highest peak in Attica lying directly to the north of Athens.

STREPSIADES:
By Zeus! The Illustrious ones themselves, they're everywhere, all
around us!

SOCRATES:
And to think that you never knew they were goddesses, you had
no faith.

STREPSIADES:
I thought they were just a load of old vapor, all drizzle and fog!   330

SOCRATES:
Exactly, because you were unaware that they cultivate a slew of
sophisticated scholars;
Prophets from the colonies, atmospheric therapists, long-haired
loungers with jangling jewelry,
creators of complex, convoluted compositions, ethereal, immaterial,
vacuous visionaries!
Intangible, insubstantial idleness sustained by waxing lyrical
about the Clouds!

STREPSIADES:
Oh, I see! That's why they utter things like "the menacing storm
clouds advance, edged   335
with silver linings" and then call them "the billowing locks of
hundred-headed Typhon,"
"furious gusts," "sky-borne cisterns," "jagged clawed birds
soaring through the air,"
and sing about "torrents pouring down from rain filled clouds,"
and for that load
of hot air they get rewarded with beautiful fillets of fish and
lovely little roasted thrushes!

334: Aristophanes may be describing Lampon the Prophet, Hippocrates of
Cos, the wealthy young students of the sophists and dithyrambic poets
(***331–34 Sophisticated scholars**).

336: Typhon was a mythological hundred-headed monster associated with
violent storm winds.

339: A victorious poet was given a festive banquet by his producer
following the performances.

SOCRATES:

340   Just think, it's all due to the Clouds.

STREPSIADES:

    But if they are supposed to be Clouds, why do they look like women?
    What happened? The Clouds up in the sky don't look like that.

SOCRATES:

    Well, what do they look like?

STREPSIADES:

    I don't really know just how to describe them exactly. Like a flock
       of woolly sheepskin rugs,
    certainly not like women. I've never seen a Cloud with a nose before.

SOCRATES:

345   Really? Then answer this one question.

STREPSIADES:

    Ask away.

SOCRATES:

    Have you ever looked up at the Clouds and thought that they
       seemed
    to assume the shape of, say a centaur, perhaps a leopard, or even a
       bull?

STREPSIADES:

    I have, but so what?

SOCRATES:

    The Clouds can assume any form they please. If they should
       happen to look down and spy
    some long-haired, unkempt uncivilized type, say the son of
       Xenophantus, for example,
    then they assume the form of a centaur in recognition of his true
350   heart's desire.

350: This probably refers to the poet Hieronymus, ridiculed in *Acharnians*
(lines 388–90) for his long hair. Centaurs, the half-man, half-horse creatures
of mythology, were often portrayed as possessing rampant sexual appetites.

STREPSIADES:
Ha! Then what if they see that fraudster, Simon, who robbed the
public funds?

SOCRATES:
Then they assume his true likeness and turn into wolves.

STREPSIADES:
Oh! Now I know why they looked like a herd of deer the other day.
They must have recognized Cleonymus, the shield-shedder, for
the cowardly bastard that he is.

SOCRATES:
Precisely, and now they have obviously just seen Cleisthenes,
hence they become women!   355

STREPSIADES:
Oh, hail divine ladies! Please do for me what you do for others,
sing a song to reach the very heights of heaven.

CHORUS:
(*To Strepsiades*) Hail, O geriatric one, you who quest for artful words.
(*To Socrates*) Hail priest of pedantic prattle, what would you bid
us do?
There are only two ethereal experts we hearken to: 360
Prodicus for his sheer wisdom and knowledge,
and you, for the way you strut around like a grand gander,*
roll your eyes, go barefoot, endure all, and hold such high opinions.

351: Probably a corrupt minor politician in the circle of Cleon (*351 Simon).

354: A minor Athenian politician nicknamed the "shield-dropper" by
Aristophanes for alleged cowardice in battle.

355: Cleisthenes was frequently ridiculed in Aristophanic comedy for his
effeminate manner and lack of a beard. He appears as a character in
Aristophanes' *Thesmophoriazusae* (lines 575–654).

361: A renowned sophist known for his teachings on the intricacies of
language and their effective use in argument. He was operating in Athens
around the same time as Socrates and held radical views concerning the
birth of the cosmos (see *Birds* lines 690–92).

STREPSIADES:
   Good Earth! What vocals! Wondrous, sacred, marvelous!

SOCRATES:
   You see, these are the only true gods, everything else is utter
365   nonsense.

STREPSIADES:
   What about Zeus? How can Olympian Zeus not be a god?

SOCRATES:
   Zeus? Don't be absurd! Zeus doesn't exist.

STREPSIADES:
   What are you saying? Who is it that makes rain, then?

SOCRATES:
   Why, the Clouds of course! I'll prove it to you. Does it ever rain
370   without Clouds? No, and you would have thought that Zeus could
   have made rain on his own if he so desired, without the help of
   the Clouds.

STREPSIADES:
   And I always thought it was Zeus pissing through a sieve!
   You certainly have a way with words, that makes complete sense.
   But hold on, who makes the thunder that makes me shake in teror?

SOCRATES:
375   It is just the Clouds rocking in the sky.

STREPSIADES:
   Is nothing sacred! How do they do that?

368: Zeus was known as the Sky Father. He was said to cause the rain,
thunder, and lightning, and many of his rituals originated in a desire to
control the weather and pray for rain.

375: Similar theories were held by the earlier philosophers, Heraclitus and
Anaxagoras.

SOCRATES:

> Simple. When they become completely saturated with moisture, they are forced
> by Necessity to begin to oscillate to and fro. Every now and again they ram each other
> and of course, being packed with precipitation, CRASH! A cloudburst!

STREPSIADES:

> But surely someone must force them to move in the first place. That must be Zeus.

SOCRATES:

> Not at all, it is the whirling of the Celestial Basin!   *380*

STREPSIADES:

> Basin? So Zeus is no more and Basin is king now, is he?
> But you haven't explained who it is that makes the thunder.

SOCRATES:

> Listen! The Clouds become full of water and crash into each other, thus they emit a thundering sound because of their sheer density.

STREPSIADES:

> Do you seriously expect me to believe that?   *385*

SOCRATES:

> Then allow me to demonstrate, using you as my example. Have you ever been
> at the Panathenaea Festival, and eaten too much soup? What happened?
> Your stomach suddenly became upset and started to rumble, yes?

378: "Necessity" is *ananké*, the personification of the compelling force of nature (***378 Necessity**).

380: The Greek has *dinos*, a large bowl used for mixing wine and also a term that means "vortex" (***380 Celestial Basin**).

381: Zeus became king of the gods by overthrowing his father Cronus.

387: A public festival held in honor of Athena each year with the Great Panathenaea occurring once every four years.

STREPSIADES:

Yes, by Apollo. It grumbles and groans with all that soup sloshing
around,
and then it makes a noise that sounds just like thunder. First of all
it's just a little splutter . . . Phuurrrt! Then it gets a bit louder
390   . . . PHHUuuuurrtt!
And when I finally get to take a shit, it really thunders just like
those clouds . . .
. . . PHHHAAAARRRRAAARRRAAATTT!

SOCRATES:

My dear old fellow, if a tiny stomach such as yours can emit such
a fart,
just think what a colossal thunder the vast atmosphere can
produce.

STREPSIADES:

Yes, thunder and farter, they even sound the same.
395   But what about those flashing, fiery shafts of lightning that can burn
us to a crisp or at the least give us a good grilling every now and then?
Surely that is Zeus' instrument against oath-breakers.

SOCRATES:

You blithering, prehistoric, pre-cronian old fool!
If Zeus smites oath-breakers, why has he not incinerated Simon,
Cleonymus, or Theorus? They couldn't break more oaths if they
tried!
Instead he strikes the temple at Cape Sunium and turns his own
400   oak trees to charcoal.
Everyone knows that an oath as solid as oak can't be broken.
What was he thinking?

394: In Greek, *brontê* and *pordê*. Etymology was an area of interest for the
sophists, reduced to cheap toilet humor by Strepsiades.

398: Cronus was the father of Zeus, and his name a byword for archaic times.

399: Theorus was a minor politician in the circle of Cleon; he is vilified as a
flatterer in *Wasps* (lines 42–51).

400: A promontory on the southeastern point of Attica jutting out into the
Aegean Sea.

401: The oak tree was sacred to Zeus. The god's presence at his shrine in
Dodona was represented by a holy oak tree.

STREPSIADES:
I don't know, but it all sounds very convincing. So what's a
thunderbolt then?

SOCRATES:
When an arid gust is blown up above and becomes trapped inside
the clouds,
it tends to inflate them rather like a bladder; the sheer volume of *405*
air causes
the clouds to explode, and the compressed hot wind is forced out
with such
terrific energy that in the process it bursts into spontaneous flame.*

STREPSIADES:
The exact same thing happened to me once at the Diasia feast.
I was cooking a nice big sausage for the family, and I completely *410*
forgot to prick it. Well, it swelled right up and suddenly BANG!
It blew up right in my face, and showered me with hot blood
and fat!

CHORUS:
You come craving knowledge of the highest kind
So the Greeks will call you Athens' mastermind. *415*
If you possess a brain fit for cogitation
And can suffer cold, stress, and deprivation.
If you can pace about and stand for hours
Not drink nor train by sheer willpower,
If you hold the clever soul in high regard,
Battling by the tongue will not be hard. *420*

STREPSIADES:
My mind never rests, I'm as tough as old boots.
I've a mean, lean stomach, and I can live on roots.
Fear not, there's nothing that this body can't handle;
I'm ready to temper my spirit upon your anvil!

408: A festival sacred to Zeus Meilichios ("the kindly one").

SOCRATES:
And do you repudiate all other gods, except those we venerate,
the holy trinity of Chaos, Clouds, and a confident tongue?

STREPSIADES:
425   I wouldn't even speak to a god if I met one, and you won't catch me
sacrificing, pouring libations, or burning incense on any of their
altars.

CHORUS:
Then tell us, what is it you would like us to do for you? We will
not fail you,
not if you pay us due honor and respect and come in search of
knowledge.

STREPSIADES:
Reverend ladies! It's just a tiny little thing that I ask of you;
430   I wish to be the finest speaker in all of Greece, a hundred times over!

CHORUS:
So be it. From this day henceforth no man shall ever pass
more motions in the public assembly than you . . .

STREPSIADES:
No, no, no! I'm not interested in politics and carrying on in the
assembly!
I want to twist Justice around and escape the clutches of my
creditors.

CHORUS:
Then you will have your heart's desire, it is but a small thing you
435   require.
Just place yourself into the hands of our leading devotees.

STREPSIADES:
I'll do it! I have to! I've got no choice, you see!
The horses and my marriage will be the death of me!

So here I am, take me now, I'm yours!
440   *Beat me, bruise me, it's in a very good cause.*

I'll starve, not bathe, shiver, shake, and freeze,
Feel free to tan my hide as often as you please!

I'll do anything to avoid the paying of my debts,
And men will come to realize my newly won assets.
I'll be dangerous, mad, and devil-may-care,   445
A low-down dirty liar, driven to despair!

A courthouse junkie blessed with the gift of gab,
A barrack-room lawyer and a filthy, oily rag!
A chiseler, a shyster, a bullshitter and cheat,   450
A miscreant, a twister, and a master of deceit!

Feed me on chop logic, I'll feast on your split hairs,
And all those who meet me should take extra care.
So now I've told you what it is I yearn to be,   455
Serve me to your students and make mincemeat out of me!

CHORUS:
  I can't help but admire
  his sheer strength of character.
  Let me tell you this,
  If you learn your lessons well,   460
  Your very name will reach up
  to resound in the heights of heaven!

STREPSIADES:
  Then what lies in store for me?

CHORUS:
  For the rest of your days you will be
  the most blessed and envied of all men.   465

STREPSIADES:
  Really?

CHORUS:
  Of course!
  Crowds will gather at your door

clamoring for any opportunity
470   to actually get to talk to you.
They'll all come in supplication,
seeking your sage advice.
You'll help them to decide vitally important
and extravagantly expensive issues,
475   issues suited to such an intellect as yours.
Now to enroll this old man in our educational program;
it is time to stimulate his mind and test his knowledge.

SOCRATES:
So, tell me a little about yourself.
I need to understand your particular personality traits.
480   Then I can correctly determine the best tactics to deploy.

STREPSIADES:
Tactics? Are you planning to lay siege to me?

SOCRATES:
No, no, I just want to analyze you a little.
Now then, are you in possession of a powerful memory?

STREPSIADES:
Well, that all depends. If someone owes me money,
485   it is quite superb, but if, on the other hand, I owe money,
then I'm afraid it has a tendency to let me down.

SOCRATES:
Then perhaps you have a particular penchant for oral recitation?

STREPSIADES:
(Laughing) Me? I'm certainly reticent to pay my debts!

SOCRATES:
Look, how on earth do you expect to learn anything?

STREPSIADES:
Oh, don't be such a worrier, I'll get the hang of it.

SOCRATES:
All right then, make sure that whenever I throw out some juicy bits

of heavenly wisdom that you snatch them up right away. *490*

STREPSIADES:
(*Laughing*) What do you take me for, a dog?

SOCRATES:
You utter, uneducated barbarian oaf!
We may well have to beat some sense into this old fool.
Tell me, what would you do if someone were to hit you?

STREPSIADES:
I'd fall over! And I'd stay down too, at least until a witness *495*
came along. Then I'd go and file assault charges
and get a hefty out-of-court settlement or some nice damages!

SOCRATES:
Remove your outer garment.

STREPSIADES:
What for, am I in trouble already?

SOCRATES:
No, all new initiates must disrobe.

STREPSIADES:
But, I promise I won't steal anything inside.

SOCRATES:
Just take the damn thing off, will you! *500*

(*Strepsiades takes off his tunic and gives it to Socrates, leaving
him naked except for a loincloth.*)

STREPSIADES:
If I work really hard and attend to my studies,
which of your followers can I ever hope to be like?

499: Under Athenian law a citizen could search the house of a suspected
thief. However, the person had to first remove his cloak to prove that he was
not attempting to plant any incriminating evidence.

SOCRATES:
You should try to be like Chaerephon.

STREPSIADES:
Good gods no, I'll be as good as dead!

SOCRATES:
505   Will you please stop jabbering away.
Get a move on and follow me!

STREPSIADES:
All right, all right, but at least put a honey cake in my hand,
I'm scared, it's like descending into Trophonius' grotto.

SOCRATES:
Stop dilly-dallying at the door and come on!

*(Enter Socrates and Strepsiades into the Pondertorium through the
stage left door.)*

CHORUS:
510   *Good luck to this brave soul*
Embarking on his quest,
Though he's old and gray
I know he'll do his best.
A dyed-in-the-wool spirit
515   *Dipping into new ideas,*
Such a radical education
For a man of advanced years.

[Parabasis]

*(The chorus leader addresses the audience, speaking for
Aristophanes.)*

508: A legendary master builder who had an oracle near Lebadea in
Boeotia. Visitors performed various initiation rites before descending into a
mysterious subterranean passage armed with a honey cake to placate the
serpents who were said to guard the cave (**508 Trophonius**).

CHORUS:
  Dear audience, allow me to speak candidly for a moment.
  It is time to hear the truth, sworn by Dionysus, the very deity
  that nurtured my rare talent and raised me to win great dramatic
    victories.   *520*
  I thought that you were an intelligent audience, I thought that
    you would
  truly enjoy this, the most intellectual of all my comedies.
  I sweated night and day over a hot script to serve up to you
  the very first taste of the fruits of my labor. But look what happened.
  I was utterly defeated, thwarted by those other vile, despicable hacks! *525*
  And it is you people who must bear the blame for this disgrace,
  for you should have known better. I did it all for you, and just
    look how you chose
  to repay me! But never fear, I will always be here for those with
    the good taste
  to fully appreciate the quality of my work. It was here, in this very
    theatre,
  that my tale of the righteous boy and the little bugger was so very
    well received.   *530*
  It is true that I was not yet of an age to mother properly such a
    child, and so I exposed
  my prodigy to be adopted by another in my stead. Then you, dear
    audience, you all
  became its foster parents, it was you who nurtured it, you raised it.
  Ever since then I have held you all in the highest esteem, and I always
  swore by your sound judgment and prudent wisdom. And now
    like Electra,   *535*
  this comedy comes searching, hoping, seeking an audience equal
    in wit and intelligence,

525: This text of *Clouds* seems to have been revised. The original production placed third at the festival of Dionysus in 421.

530: Probably *Banqueters* (427), Aristophanes' first play, which placed second.

535: Electra was the daughter of Agamemnon and Clytemnestra, a famous figure in both myth and drama. Aeschylus, Sophocles, and Euripides all produced plays about Electra longing for the return of her brother, Orestes.

and like the hair on Orestes' head, she'll know them when she
sees them!

Contemplate for a moment, if you will, the value of her discreet
sensibilities.

She does not dangle one of those huge, red-tipped appendages
540   between her legs to get cheap laughs from the children among you.*

She doesn't make rude jibes at the expense of bald men, and she
categorically refuses*

to perform any kind of suggestive dances. You will never see her
leading actor

dressed up as an old man, running around, hitting all and sundry
with a stick

to divert your attention from the poor quality of the rotten old
jokes! What's more

you will certainly not encounter anybody charging onstage with
flaming torches,

shouting Oh! Oh! No, this play comes here today trusting only in
545   itself and its poetry,*

and I, the playwright, am cast from the same mold. I have always
been bold

(bold, not bald—I know I'm bald!), and I have never ever
attempted to bamboozle you

by rehashing the same tired old material time and time again. No,
I devote

every strain of my poetic fiber to the invention of brand new,
cutting-edge comedy.

Every play has something different, something innovative,
vivacious, and skillful.

When Cleon was at the peak of his powers, I slugged him in the
550   stomach,

but I never hit the man when he was down. But just look at my
rivals and how they

treated Hyperbolus, they walked all over him, not to mention the
punishment they

537: Orestes proved his identity to Electra with a lock of hair in Aeschylus'
The Libation Bearers (lines 229–30).

550: Aristophanes caricatures the demagogue Cleon in *Wasps*.

552: Hyperbolus became prominent in Athenian public life after the death
of Cleon in 422.

dealt out to his poor old mother! It all started with Eupolis and
that dreadful farce
of his, *Maricas*, blatant plagiarism! A disgusting imitation of my
Knights with the totally
unnecessary addition of an inebriated old hag crudely gyrating in
the dances.*   555
The very same character, might I add, that we saw Phrynichus present
in his comedy about the women being fed to the sea creature!
Then came Hermippus, and his vicious attacks on Hyperbolus.
Soon everyone jumped on the Hyperbolus band wagon and were
happily
dishing out the dirt, and worst of all stealing all my best eel gags!   560
If you find that kind of drivel amusing, you will never fully
appreciate my work,
but those who enjoy my comedic innovations will be considered
wise in years to come.

Zeus the highest god of all,
Greatest ruler, hear our call.

Come, Poseidon, with trident flashing,   565
From salty depths with breakers crashing.

The sky-father that witnessed our birth
Most sacred nurturer of life on earth.   570

The charioteer who fills our days,
With the light, heat, and brilliant rays.

553: Eupolis was one of the most highly regarded Athenian comic poets.
His work survives only in fragments, but he is known to have produced his
first play in 429 and won at least seven victories. Hyperbolus' mother
appeared in his *Maricas* of 421.

557: A comic dramatist and contemporary of Aristophanes. Evidently he
had produced a comic farce based on the Andromeda myth.

558: The comic dramatist Hermippus had produced a play called *Bread
Sellers* which featured Hyperbolus and his mother.

560: In *Knights* (lines 864–67) Aristophanes said Cleon's politics were like a
fisherman stirring up the mud to get the eels to bite.

571: This is Helios, the sun god, who drives his chariot from the east to the
west, bringing light.

To god and mortal, great power advance,
We call you all to join our dance!

(The Clouds address the audience.)

Attention please, audience! It is time to prick your collective
575   conscience.
You have performed us a great disservice, and we are here to
    chastise you for it!
No deity gives more to this city than we, and yet you fail to pay us
    the slightest respect!
We are the ones who are ever-present, and we constantly have
    your best interests
at heart, but you never pour us any libations or even offer a single
    sacrifice!
When you are about to embark on some futile armed campaign,
580   we bellow noisily
and send sheets of rain. When you were holding elections for
    general and chose
that damned Paphlagonian tanner, we frowned down and
    thundered our dissent.
"Such sheets of fire, such bursts of horrid thunder." Even the
    moon reversed*
her course, and the very sun in the sky snuffed his great wick and
585   announced
that he would not rekindle his heavenly light if you nominated
    Cleon as General!
But in spite of everything, you still went ahead and voted for the man!
It has been said that bad decisions run rife in this city, and yet
    somehow the gods
always conspire to make everything turn out for the best. It is the
    same in this instance,

581: It seems from Aristophanes' *Acharnians* (lines 170–73) that a meeting
of the assembly could be canceled due to rain. Thunder was also
traditionally viewed as giving voice to the displeasure of the gods.

582: Aristophanes' nickname for Cleon as used in *Knights*. Cleon's family
may have owned a tanning factory.

586: Cleon was elected as one of the ten generals around February 424, and
an eclipse occurred in March (Thucydides 4.52.1).

for there is a simple solution to turn this terrible error of judgment
   to your advantage.   *590*
Just go ahead and indict that gannet Cleon on charges of fraud
   and embezzlement,
clap him in the stocks, and lock him up. Lo and behold, out of
   your previous folly
shall come your salvation, everything will be as before,
back the way things were, to the very great benefit of your city.

Come, Phoebus Apollo, lord of Delos,   *595*
Leave Cynthus' rocks and come to us.

Come, Artemis, leave your house of gold,
Worshipped by Lydian daughters age-old.

Goddess of the Aegis, protector of our city,   *600*
Lady Athena, held in highest sanctity.

From Parnassus' towering heights,
Setting ablaze his pine torch light,

The Bacchants of Delphi, wild and joyous,   *605*
Come, festive god, come, Dionysus.

LEADER:
   When we were on our way here, we happened to meet the Moon,
   who told us to relay her benedictions to the Athenians and their allies.
   However, she also informed us that she is very cross with you   *610*
   and that you have treated her with disrespect, despite all
   the wonderful things she has done for you all. Just think, she saves
   you at least a drachma a month for all the torches you have no
      need of.
   She's heard you telling your houseboys, "Don't bother with the lamp
   tonight, my lad, the moonlight's nice and bright."   *615*
   She does that for you and a lot more besides! She also informed us
   that she is most displeased with all this fiddling about with the
      lunar cycle,
   she says it is playing absolute havoc with the calendar, and she
      has received numerous
   complaints from angry gods who have been cheated out of their
      due festival days!*

To top it all, on sacred sacrificial days you are going around,
620   torturing people
and sitting in court passing judgment when you should be
worshipping.
There have even been times when the gods were partaking in a
solemn memorial
service to Memnon or Sarpedon while you lot were pouring
libations, drinking
and cavorting about all over the city—disgraceful! That is why
Hyperbolus,
your elected religious remembrancer, had his wreath removed by
625   the gods.
Now he knows that you should arrange your dates in concordance
with the moon!

(Enter Socrates from the stage left door.)

SOCRATES:
By Breath, by Chaos, by Air!
I have never before encountered such a feeble-minded,
imbecilic, slow-witted country bumpkin in all my life!
630   He forgets the tiniest scraps of knowledge
before he's even had a chance to learn them!

(Calling into the Pondertorium)

Strepsiades! Come on out here, into the light,
Hurry up, and bring the couch with you.*

*(Enter Strepsiades, still seminaked, from the stage left door
carrying a small couch. Like Socrates, he is now barefoot.)*

623: Both warriors from the Trojan War. Memnon was the king of the
Ethiopians and the son of Eos (Dawn) and Tithonus. The morning dew was
regarded as Dawn crying for her slain son who was killed by Achilles.
Sarpedon was the son of Zeus and Laodamia and was killed by Patroclus.
Zeus was so devastated by his son's death that he caused blood to rain
down from the sky.

625: A remembrancer served on the Amphictyonic council, which decided
sacred matters at Delphi. Perhaps a freak gust of wind had swept away
Hyperbolus' official wreath at such an occasion.

627: The act of drawing breath was connected with the intellect by both
Heraclitus and Diogenes of Apollonia.

STREPSIADES:
No need, the flea-infested thing can get up and walk out on its own!

SOCRATES:
Put it down over there and listen carefully. 635

STREPSIADES:
All right.

SOCRATES:
Good, let's get started. Which facet of your intellect do you wish
to develop?
Perhaps you would like to use this opportunity to master a subject
you never had
the opportunity to learn before? Meter? Rhythm? Scales?

STREPSIADES:
Scales! Only the other day that bastard grain merchant
fiddled me out of a full two measures! 640

SOCRATES:
Not those kind of scales, you idiot! I'm attempting to engage you
in a discussion
on music and poetry. Now, consider which measure is more
aesthetically pleasing,
the three-quarter beat or the four-quarter beat?

STREPSIADES:
Personally, I think the pint takes some beating!

SOCRATES:
Will you stop babbling such utter nonsense!

STREPSIADES:
It's not nonsense, everyone knows four quarts makes a pint! 645

SOCRATES:
Oh damn you! You illiterate uneducated peasant!
Let's at least see if you can learn something about rhythm.

STREPSIADES:
Rhythm? How is learning about rhythm going to buy me barley?

SOCRATES:
A detailed knowledge of rhythm enables you to socialize effectively in polite

company and seem refined and cultured. You'll know all about
650   martial modes
and dactylic meter . . .

> *(Strepsiades looks confused.)*

> > > Beating the rhythm with your fingers!*

STREPSIADES:
I know how to beat with my fingers, by Zeus!

SOCRATES:
You do? Tell me about it.

STREPSIADES:
Well when I was a young lad it was this . . .

> *(Strepsiades grabs and shuffles his phallus.)*

SOCRATES:
655   Gods! You are nothing but a village idiot!

STREPSIADES:
You're the idiot, I don't want to learn any of this stuff.

SOCRATES:
Well, what DO you want to learn?

STREPSIADES:
The other thing, you know *(whispering):* the Wrong Argument.

SOCRATES:
That's an advanced class, you can't just start there, you have to
master the basics first,

such as the correct gender affiliation of certain types of quadrupedic
  livestock.*

STREPSIADES:
  Livestock! I'm an expert. Let's see, masculine: *660*
  ram, billy-goat, bull, dog, chicken . . .

SOCRATES:
  And the feminine?

STREPSIADES:
  Ewe, nanny-goat, cow, bitch, chicken . . .

SOCRATES:
  Aha! You called both the male and the female chicken.
  You can't do that!

STREPSIADES:
  What do you mean?

SOCRATES:
  You said "chicken" and "chicken."

STREPSIADES:
  By Poseidon, you're right! Well, what should I have said?   *665*

SOCRATES:
  Chicken . . . and chickeness!

STREPSIADES:
  Chickeness? That's a good one, by Air!
  For just that single piece of learning
  I should fill your meal-kneader with barley oats.

662: The Greek word *alektruôn* was used for both the cock and the hen.

669: A *cardopus* was a troughlike kneading tray with a large pestle that was
used like a rolling pin (*671 Meal-kneader). Barley was a cheap food but
also part of many sacred festivals and initiation rites.

SOCRATES:

670   You've done it again, said another one. You used the masculine form
       for meal-kneader, but it really should be feminine.

STREPSIADES:
       What? I made a meal-kneader masculine?

SOCRATES:
       Yes, just like Cleonymus.

STREPSIADES:
       What do you mean?

SOCRATES:
       Meal-kneader and Cleonymus are treated in the same manner.

STREPSIADES:

675   But Socrates, Cleonymus doesn't even own a meal kneader.
       His "needs" are met by having his oats delivered by the back door,*
       if you, eh, know what I mean! What should I call it from now on?

SOCRATES:
       The feminine form, that is "fe-meal kneader."

STREPSIADES:
       So a meal-kneader needs a female to be a fe-meal kneader?

SOCRATES:
       Exactly.

STREPSIADES:

680   I see, so I should have said, Cleonymus never needed a female?

SOCRATES:
       Yes. Well then, we must still educate you on proper names.
       You need to know which are masculine and which are feminine.

671: The word *cardopus* is feminine, although it appears to have a masculine
ending.

STREPSIADES:
I know which are feminine all right.

SOCRATES:
Go on then.

> (*Strepsides lustfully imagines a group of well-known Athenian beauties.*)

STREPSIADES:
Lysilla (*Wow wee!*), Philinna (*Oh yeah!*), Cleitagora (*Hubba, hubba*), and Demetria (*Ow!*).

SOCRATES:
And the masculine names? 685

> (*He imagines a collection of effeminate young men.*)

STREPSIADES:
There's plenty: Philoxenus (*Luvvie!*), Melesias (*Big Boy!*), Amynias (*Hello sailor!*) . . .

SOCRATES:
Those are hardly masculine!

STREPSIADES:
You don't think they're masculine?

SOCRATES:
Absolutely not. If you saw Amynias, just how would you call out to him?

STREPSIADES:
Like this. "Coo-ee! Coo-ee! Amynia luvvie! Amynia darling!" 690

684: All of these seem to be fairly common women's names; however, the scholia cite them as prostitutes. Cleitagora is mentioned in this context in *Wasps* (lines 1245-47).

686: Philoxenus ("Guest-lover") was regarded by Old Comedy as a homosexual, Melesias is unknown, and Amynias is attacked several times in *Wasps* as a corrupt good-for-nothing and freeloader (see *Wasps* 74–76, 466, and 1267–70).

SOCRATES:
I rest my case. You are clearly calling out to him like a woman,
and what's more, "Amynia" is feminine.

STREPSIADES:
That's what the old poof gets for dodging the draft.
But everyone knows Amynias is an old woman, I don't need to be
taught that.

SOCRATES:
Be quiet by Zeus! Now lie down on the couch there.

STREPSIADES:
What for?

SOCRATES:
695   You need to concentrate on personal matters.

STREPSIADES:
No, I'm begging you! Don't make me lie down there. I can just as
easily
do my personal concentrating on the bare earth!

SOCRATES:
I'm sorry, you simply have no choice.

STREPSIADES:
Oh no! Those fleas are going to have a field day feasting on me!

(Exit Socrates through the stage left door.)

CHORUS:
700   *So philosophize and cogitate,*
Intellectualize and ruminate.
Twist your thoughts, your mind must bend,
Through mental blocks and each dead end.
Let ideas jump and concepts fly,
705   *Don't let sweet sleep close your eyes.*

STREPSIADES:
Oh! Woe! Oh! Woe!

CHORUS:
What pains thee, art thou smitten?

STREPSIADES:
Misery! Agony! I'm being bitten!
They're leaping off this bed and biting
Like Corinthians fleeing from the fighting!   710
They've been gnawing on my bones all day,
They're sucking all my blood away!
They've champed my bollocks all red raw,
My poor old arse has never felt this sore!
These bugs will chew me half to death . . .   715

CHORUS:
I suggest you give that moaning a rest!

STREPSIADES:
Some hope you are, what bad advice!
I've lost money and health for a load of lice!
My very soul is bruised and beaten,
My clothes and shoes are all moth eaten.   720
So I sing to keep my spirits high,
But it's all over now, the end is nigh!

   (Enter Socrates through the stage left door.)

SOCRATES:
What are you doing? You are supposed to be contemplating.

STREPSIADES:
I am, by Poseidon.

SOCRATES:
And just what, pray, have you been contemplating?

707: The high language is a parody from tragedy, perhaps Euripides'
Hecuba, produced just a year earlier.

710: "Corinthians" seems to have been an Athenian slang term for
"bedbugs" or "fleas," derived from a simple pun on *koreis* (bugs) and
Korinthioi (Corinthians).

STREPSIADES:
I've been contemplating my future, once these bugs have finished
725   me off!

SOCRATES:
Go to hell!

STREPSIADES:
Hell's right, chum! That's exactly what this is.

CHORUS:
Don't be so fainthearted, cover yourself up
and devise some fraudulent and illicit affair.

STREPSIADES:
Oh, if only instead of these lambskin covers,
730   I could get into an illicit affair!

*(Strepsiades covers himself up and lies on the couch. He wriggles
about, and then the covers rise, propped up by his phallus. Socrates
reenters.)*

SOCRATES:
All right, let's see how he's doing.
You there! Are you sleeping?

(Strepsiades pops his head out from under the fleece.)

STREPSIADES:
No, by Apollo, not me, no.

SOCRATES:
Have you been able to get a good grasp on anything?

STREPSIADES:
Eh . . . well, no, not really.

729: Veiling the head in a lamb's fleece was part of the initiation rites of the
Eleusinian Mysteries.

SOCRATES:
Nothing whatsoever?

STREPSIADES:
Well, my right hand has a good grasp on my prick at the moment.

(Strepsiades removes the covers to reveal his erect phallus.)

SOCRATES:
Oh, by all the gods! Cover yourself up at once and think about
something else! 735

STREPSIADES:
But what? Tell me, Socrates, please.

SOCRATES:
No, you must discover that for yourself, then tell me what it is
you want.

STREPSIADES:
But you know very well what I want, I've told you a thousand
times:
It's my debts, I want to get out of paying them off!

SOCRATES:
All right then, cover yourself up and dissect your suppositions 740
into microscopic elements. Then consider the matter in minute
detail
thus arriving at a correct analysis derived from an orthodox
methodology.

*(Strepsiades pulls the fleece over his head and fidgets for a while
before lying down.)*

STREPSIADES:
Ohh! Ahh!

SOCRATES:
Stop fidgeting! Now, should your concept place you in a quandary
move on, free your mind, then the idea can be set in motion
once the innermost recesses of your intellect have been unlocked. 745

(Strepsiades uncovers himself.)

STREPSIADES:
My beloved Socrates!

SOCRATES:
What is it?

(Strepsiades gets up on his feet and runs toward Socrates.)

STREPSIADES:
I've thought of an illicit idea for avoiding my debts!

SOCRATES:
Do divulge.

STREPSIADES:
Tell me this . . .

SOCRATES:
What, what?

STREPSIADES:
What if I got hold of a witch from Thessaly
750   and made her magic the moon out of the sky.
I could put it away in a dressing case like a mirror,
and hide it where no one would ever find it.

SOCRATES:
But how would that help you?

STREPSIADES:
How? If I stopped the moon from rising, then I would never
755   have to pay the interest on any of my debts.

750: The reputation of Thessalian women for sorcery was proverbial.
Plato's *Gorgias* (513a) tells how they possess the power to "draw down the
moon," and Menander produced a comedy, *Thettale*, dealing with the
subject.

SOCRATES:

Why ever not?

STREPSIADES:

Because interest is always due at the end of the month, when the new moon appears!

SOCRATES:

I see, here's another situation to consider. What would you do if a lawsuit was written up against you for five talents in damages? How would you go about having the case removed from the record?

STREPSIADES:

Er, I've no idea, let me have a think about it.   760

(Strepsiades goes back under the fleece.)

SOCRATES:

Be sure not to constrict your imagination by keeping your thoughts wrapped up.
Let your mind fly through the air, but not too much. Think of your creativity
as a beetle on a string, airborne, but connected, flying, but not too high.

(He pops up from under the cover.)

STREPSIADES:

I've got it! A brilliant way of removing the lawsuit!
You're going to love this one.

SOCRATES:

Tell me more.   765

STREPSIADES:

Have you seen those pretty, see-through stones that the healers sell?*
You know, the ones they use to start fires.

763: In a popular child's game, a beetle would be tied to a stone or other heavy object and forced to fly while anchored by the string.

SOCRATES:
    You mean glass.

STREPSIADES:
    That's the stuff! If I had some glass, I could secretly position
        myself behind
    the bailiff as he writes up the case on his wax tablet. Then I could
770   aim the sun rays
    at his docket and melt away the writing so there would be no
        record of my case!

SOCRATES:
    Sweet charity! How "ingenious."

STREPSIADES:
    Great! I've managed to erase a five-talent lawsuit.

SOCRATES:
    Come on, then, chew this one over.

STREPSIADES:
775   I'm ready.

SOCRATES:
    You're in court, defending a suit, and it looks like you will surely
        lose.
    It's your turn to present your defense, and you have absolutely no
        witnesses.
    How would you effectively contest the case and, moreover, win
        the suit itself?

STREPSIADES:
    Easy!

SOCRATES:
    Let's hear it then.

772: The "Charities" or "Graces" were female deities who personified
beauty, charm, grace, the arts, and intellectual ability.

STREPSIADES:
  During the case for the prosecution,
  I would run off home and hang myself! *780*

SOCRATES:
  What are you talking about?

STREPSIADES:
  By all the gods, it's foolproof! How can anybody sue me when
    I'm dead?

SOCRATES:
  This is preposterous! I've had just about enough of this!
  You'll get no more instruction from me.

STREPSIADES:
  But Socrates, in the name of heaven, why not?

SOCRATES:
  Because if I do manage to get something through to you, it is
    instantly *785*
  forgotten. Here, I'll prove it. What was the first thing I taught you?

STREPSIADES:
  Mmmm, the first lesson, hang on, let me think, what was that, uh,
  something female where we scatter our oats, oh I don't know!

SOCRATES:
  You fossilized, forgetful old fool! Just piss off! *790*

  (Exit Socrates in disgust through the stage left door.)

STREPSIADES:
  Oh no! I'm finished. This is terrible!
  If I don't learn tongue-twisting, then I'm lost without a hope!
  Clouds! You have to help me out. What can I do?

CHORUS:
  You have a grownup son, don't you?
  If you take our advice, *795*
  you will send him to take your place.

STREPSIADES:
Yes, I've a son, a refined, lovely lad, but he's not interested
in higher education. What else can I do?

CHORUS:
He's your son, is he not? Who is master of your house?

STREPSIADES:
800   Well, he's a passionate, spirited boy from a fine family,
the house of Coesyra, no less. But you're right, it's high time
I set him straight, and if he says no, then he's out on his ear
once and for all. Wait for me, I won't be long.

*(Exit Strepsiades through the stage right door as the chorus
serenades Socrates.)*

CHORUS:
Now it is clear, once and for all
805   *The great benefits we bring to you,*
For this man is at your beck and call
To us alone, your prayers are due.

You've created one hysterical man,
810   *His excitement cannot be contained.*
Now quickly take him for all you can
For luck can change and drain away.

*(Enter Pheidippides from the stage right door, chased by
Strepsiades.)*

STREPSIADES:
Get out! By Vapor, out of my house, once and for all.
815   Go and eat your uncle Megacles out of house and home!

PHEIDIPPIDES:
Father, whatever is the matter?
You are clearly insane, by Zeus!

814: Strepsiades' own version of Socrates' "by Air" (lines 627 and 667).

STREPSIADES:
> Listen to you, "By Zeus!" How childish!
> Fancy believing in Olympian Zeus at your age.

PHEIDIPPIDES:
> What on earth is so funny?   *820*

STREPSIADES:
> You are, a young child like you with such old-fashioned ideas,
> it's really quite ridiculous. But listen, come here, I want to reveal
> something to you. When you understand, then, and only then, my son,
> will you truly be a man. But you must ensure that no one else
> knows this.

PHEIDIPPIDES:
> Well, I'm here. Now what is it?   *825*

STREPSIADES:
> Did you or did you not just swear to Zeus?

PHEIDIPPIDES:
> I did.

STREPSIADES:
> Now you'll see the benefits of education.
> Pheidippides, there is no Zeus!

PHEIDIPPIDES:
> What!

STREPSIADES:
> Zeus is overthrown! Basin is king now!

PHEIDIPPIDES:
> Ha! What rot!

STREPSIADES:
> It's the truth.

PHEIDIPPIDES:
> I don't believe you, who told you this nonsense?

STREPSIADES:

830   Socrates the Melian and Chaerephon,
       and he's an expert in the true path of . . . fleas.

PHEIDIPPIDES:
       Oh dear, your insanity is at a really advanced stage
       if you have begun to follow the views of those maniacs.

STREPSIADES:
       How dare you say such things! These are brilliant men
835   with superb minds. They live a simple frugal life and refuse
       to cut their hair, use soap, or set foot in a bathhouse.
       But you, you've been taking yourself and my money to the cleaners
       for years, scrubbing away as if I was dead and buried!
       Come on, hurry up, you have to go and learn in my place.

PHEIDIPPIDES:
840   What for? There's nothing even vaguely useful they could teach me.

STREPSIADES:
       Nothing useful? What about all worldly knowledge, eh?
       You could start off by learning what an imbecile you are.
       Hang on, I've just had a thought. Wait here!

       (*Exit Strepsiades through the stage right door.*)

PHEIDIPPIDES:
       Dear me! Father is clearly completely deranged, what should I do?
845   I could have him tried in court and found legally incompetent,*
       or perhaps I had better book the undertaker right away.

       (*Enter Strepsiades through the stage right door holding two
       identical chickens.*)

STREPSIADES:
       Now then, tell me what you would call this?

830: Strepsiades confuses Socrates with "the Melian," Diagoras of Melos,
an atheist who openly scorned traditional religious views. He was
eventually condemned to death (see *Birds* lines 1072–74).

(Strepsiades holds up one of the chickens.)

PHEIDIPPIDES:
A chicken.

STREPSIADES:
Very good. And what would you call this?

(Strepsiades holds up the other chicken.)

PHEIDIPPIDES:
A chicken.

STREPSIADES:
Really? You would call them both by the same name, eh?
Now you really are being stupid. Here let me show you
so you will know next time you are asked; this one here   *850*
is indeed called a "chicken". . . but this is a "chickeness."

PHEIDIPPIDES: *(Laughing)*
"Chickeness!" Is that an example of the "worldly knowledge"
that you learned in that house of stupid old clods?

*(Strepsiades throws the chickens off and starts to lead Pheidippides
to the stage left door.)*

STREPSIADES:
It is, but son, I couldn't remember most of the stuff they taught,
every time I learned something I would forget it, I'm just too old
and . . .   *855*

PHEIDIPPIDES:
That's why you've lost the clothes off your back, is it?

STREPSIADES:
They're not lost, just donated to my educational endowment.

PHEIDIPPIDES:
And just where are your shoes, you gullible old idiot?

STREPSIADES:
> To quote Pericles, "They were spent on necessary expenses."
860 Come on, let's go. Do this one thing for your father, even if you
> don't agree with it. I remember when you were a little six year old,
> your little lisping voice begged me for a new toy cart as your festival*
> present, and I spent my first hard-earned obol of jury pay on you.

PHEIDIPPIDES:
865 Oh, all right then, but you'll regret this.

STREPSIADES:
> Good lad, I knew you'd be persuaded. Socrates! Come out, come
> here!
>
> *(Enter Socrates from the stage left door.)*
>
> Here is my son, as promised. I persuaded him to come along
> though he was dead set against it at first.

SOCRATES:
> No, no, no, he simply will not do, he's a mere child. He would never
> get the hang of the way we tackle things here. He just wouldn't
> grasp it.

PHEIDIPPIDES:
870 Grasp your own tackle and then go and hang yourself!*

STREPSIADES:
> Pheidippides! Watch your language in front of the teacher!

SOCRATES:
> "Graaasp?" Just listen to his infantile diction!
> What ever do you expect me to do with such flaccid lips?
> How could he learn prevarication, incrimination, and

859: Pericles had apparently used ten talents of state funds as a bribe for the
Spartans to withdraw from Athenian territory in 445. He listed this in his
annual accounts presented to the assembly as "payment for necessary
expenses."

864: Jurors received three obols a day in payment for jury service.

misrepresentation? Then again for the right course fees
it may be possible, just look what a talent bought for Hyperbolus!*

STREPSIADES:
You can do it! He'll learn, he's a natural, you'll find out!
You should have seen him when he was a little lad, gifted!
A boy genius! He'd build the most beautiful mud pies, carve
little boats, and make toy chariots out of old shoes, and you can't *880*
even begin to imagine the inventive little frogs he made from
pomegranates. I want you to teach him those two Arguments,
the Superior, whatever that is, and the Inferior, you know, the one
that can argue a wrongful case and defeat the Superior Argument.
If you can't manage both, then at least make him learn the wrong one. *885*

SOCRATES:
He can learn it from the Arguments themselves. I must be off.

(Exit Socrates through the stage left door.)

STREPSIADES:
Remember, he needs to argue his way out of all types
of legitimate lawsuits!

*(Enter the Superior Argument from the stage left door.)**

SUPERIOR:
Come out, let the audience have a look at you!
You know how much you like to show off. *890*

(Enter the Inferior Argument from the stage left door.)

INFERIOR:
Oh, "get you hence" dear *(he sees the audience)*. Ohhh! What a crowd,
the more to witness your thrashing, the better. I just love it!

SUPERIOR:
And who are you to think you can thrash me?

891: A quote from Euripides' *Telephus,* where Agamemnon quarrels with
Menelaus and tells him to "Go where you like."

INFERIOR:
Just an argument.

SUPERIOR:
An Inferior Argument.

INFERIOR:
Oh, aren't you the high and mighty one! That may be so darling,
895   but I'll still thrash you, all the same.

SUPERIOR:
Really? And just how do you plan to do that?

INFERIOR:
With innovative new ideas.

SUPERIOR:
Oh very chic, you're very fashionable aren't you,
thanks to these idiots *(indicating the audience)*.

INFERIOR:
On the contrary, they are of the highest intelligence.

SUPERIOR:
I'm going to annihilate you.

INFERIOR:
I see, how?

SUPERIOR:
900   Simply by stating my just argument.

INFERIOR:
Then let me start by defeating it with a counterargument,
because it is quite clear that Justice doesn't exist.

SUPERIOR:
Don't be ridiculous!

INFERIOR:
Well, where is she then?

SUPERIOR:
She resides with the gods on Olympus, as well you know.

INFERIOR:
Well then, if Justice lives on Olympus,
why hasn't Zeus been punished for locking up his father, mmm?*   905

SUPERIOR:
You're just spewing venom. Urghh! Get me a bucket, someone!

INFERIOR:
You're a doddering old relic.

SUPERIOR:
And you're a filthy queer!*

INFERIOR:
Your words are strewn with roses!

SUPERIOR:
Freeloader!   910

INFERIOR:
You crown me with lilies!

SUPERIOR:
Father-beater!

INFERIOR:
You're completely unaware that you're showering me with gold.

SUPERIOR:
In my day, you'd be showered with lead!

904: Hesiod describes Justice seated at the feet of Zeus on Olympus (*Works and Days* 257–59).

906: Cronus, the father of Zeus, swallowed his children to prevent them usurping him. But Rhea, Zeus' mother, substituted a stone for her son, which proved indigestible for Cronus. He vomited up the stone and the other swallowed offspring.

INFERIOR:
  Yes, I know but, my dear fellow, in these modern times we live in
  all your worse name calling just pays me greater honor!

SUPERIOR:
  You are completely contemptuous!

INFERIOR:
915 And you are absolutely archaic!

SUPERIOR:
  It's your fault that the youth of today refuses
  to attend school. You'll get your comeuppance,
  you'll see, the Athenians will realize what fools
  they've been to learn their lessons from the likes of you!

INFERIOR:
920 Pooh! You need to freshen up a bit.

SUPERIOR:
  Oh, you've been busy all right, you worthless beggar.
  You used to be the king of the scroungers,*
  gnawing on old sycophantic sayings from a tatty old swag bag.*

INFERIOR:
  How shrewd . . .

SUPERIOR:
925 How insane . . .

INFERIOR:
                    . . . all that you've said I've done.

SUPERIOR:
                              . . . the city is to support you,
  as you corrupt its young.

INFERIOR:
  Don't even think about trying to teach this boy,
  you crusty old Cronus!

SUPERIOR:
It is my duty, he needs to be saved from 930
the threat of spouting senseless gibberish.

INFERIOR:
(To Pheidippides) Come over here and ignore this reactionary old maniac.

SUPERIOR:
Keep away from him or you'll be sorry!

CHORUS:
Oh, stop all this fighting and arguing!

(Addressing the Superior Argument)

Why don't you give an account of the schooling 935
you used to give in the old days,

(Addressing the Inferior Argument)

and then you
can tell us about your new educational methods.
Then this boy can hear your conflicting arguments,
make his own mind up, and enroll in the school of his choice.

SUPERIOR:
I see no reason why not.

INFERIOR:
I'm happy to do it.

CHORUS:
Good, who would like to speak first? 940

INFERIOR:
Oh, let him go first.
I want to hear what he has to say,
then I'm going to let my innovative phraseology fly
and shoot down his arguments once and for all.
My penetrating insights are like hornets, 945
and they'll prick him blind.
And if I hear so much as a peep out of him,
he'll wish he was dead and buried!

CHORUS:
  Now our two antagonists
950 *Will decide which one is cleverest.*
  The cut and thrust of confrontation,
  A war of words and machination.
  This ideological contest
  Will decide which one is best.
955 *The end result of this demonstration*
  Is the very future of education!

  You crowned the older generation with your morality,
960 now is your chance to proudly tell us exactly what you stand for.

SUPERIOR:
  Then let me begin by explaining how education was run in the
    good old days
  when my just cause was predominant and discretion was the
    aspiration of every man.
  First, it was a given that boys should be seen and not heard and
    that students
  should attend their district schools marching through the streets
    in orderly pairs
  behind the lyre-master. Moreover, they were never allowed to
965 wear cloaks,
  even if the snow was falling as thick as porridge. These boys were
    then taught fine,
  patriotic songs, and not to rub their thighs together while seated
    in the classroom!
  Ah, yes what stirring hymns they would sing: "City-destroying
    Pallas" and "Hark I hear
  a far-off tune," and they sung strong and proud like the manly
    fathers that raised them.
  And if any boy engaged in classroom buffoonery or attempted to
970 torture the music
  by singing in the cacophonic, newfangled style of that awful lyre-
    plucker, Phrynis,

971: Phrynis introduced modulations of harmony and rhythm into the
traditional music of the *kithara* (lyre).

he was given a damned good thrashing for deliberately perverting
the Muses!
Also, while sitting in the gymnasium the boys had to keep their
legs closed in order
that they not expose the spectators to any inappropriate and
offensive sights.
When they stood up, they had to smooth the sand down where
they were sitting   *975*
so that they would not leave behind any untoward impressions of
their manhood.
No boy was permitted to oil himself below the waist, and
consequently each
had a lovely soft down on his balls like a pair of fresh, ripe
apricots . . .
They were not permitted to entice older lovers with effeminate voices,
or seductive looks, nor mince around pimping themselves out to
all and sundry!   *980*
No taking the radish head during dinner, not grabbing an elder's
celery stick,
or pulling his parsley, no nibbling on tit-bits, no giggling at the table,
no sitting with legs crossed, no . . .

INFERIOR:

What a load of archaic claptrap! Your speech, sir, reeks of rotten
old sacrificial beef,*
it is crawling with grasshoppers and hums to the antiquated
strains of Cedeides!   *985*

SUPERIOR:

Clearly you are missing the point. It was my system of student
tutoring that raised
the men who fought so bravely at Marathon. All you do is train
our young to be ashamed

985: Golden representations of grasshoppers (cicadas) were worn in the
hair of the older generation and were a symbol of the Athenians' origins as
"born from the earth of Attica." Cedeides was a dithyrambic poet who
composed in an "old-fashioned" style.

987: A famous Athenian victory over a vastly superior Persian force in 490.

of themselves and hide behind their cloaks. It grieves me to watch the war dance
at the Panathenaea and to have to see these wimpy lads who can barely lift a shield,
embarrassed at the sight of their own manly meat! It's a disgrace
990   to Athena herself!*
So come on young fellow, the choice is clear: choose me, the Superior Argument.
I'll teach you to detest hanging about in the marketplace, and to keep out of public baths.
You'll learn to be ashamed of the shameful and to burn with indignation when you are ridiculed.
You'll gracefully let your elders and betters have your seat, and you will always treat your
parents with the utmost respect, you will do nothing to harm your
995   personal virtue.
No more chasing in and out of party girls' bedrooms and running the risk of ruining your
reputation because of some harlot's love tokens. No more arguing with your father,
nor insulting his status by calling him a "crusty old fart" or "Cronus' older brother."
No, you'll come to respect all those years he spent raising you from a tiny little chick.

INFERIOR:
Oh dear me, "young fellow," if you take his advice by Dionysus
1000   you'll turn out
like those dullard sons of Hippocrates, and be forever known as a little milksop.

SUPERIOR:
Don't listen to him, you'll be forever in the wrestling school, your bronzed body

---

1001: Hippocrates was elected to the Athenian generalship in 426–25. He died at the battle of Delium in 424, leaving three sons, Demophon, Pericles, and Telesippus, who were regarded as uneducated morons by the comic playwrights.

glistening and hard. No wasting precious time twittering away on
    absurd topics
in the marketplace, nor bickering in the courts, splitting hairs,
    arguing the toss
and wrangling over some insignificant little suit. We'll see you at
    the Academy,   *1005*
bravely racing a friend under the boughs of holy olive-trees, your
    hair festooned
with fresh cut reeds, surrounded by sweet-scented wildflowers as
    the catkins
gently fall from the willows. There, you'll not have a care in the
    world, as the trees
rustle gently in the balmy breeze, and you partake of the joys of
    spring.
This is the right way for you, my lad, and if you do what I say   *1010*
    you'll be eternally blessed
with a strapping body, a gleaming complexion,
huge shoulders, a tiny little tongue,
big buttocks, and a small cock.*
Should you choose to follow the fashion currently   *1015*
in vogue amongst the young men of this city,
then it'll be pasty skin, round shoulders,
concave chest, an enormous tongue,
no arse, a great hunk of meat, and a very long . . . turn of phrase!
He will have you believe that what should be shameful   *1020*
is beautiful, and what should be beautiful is made shameful.
Worst of all, in no time at all he'll turn you into an arse bandit
like that lecherous old queen, Antimachus.

CHORUS:

    (Addressing the Superior Argument)

    Such elevated sentiments
    Extolling high accomplishments,   *1025*

1005: A public park about a mile from the city that was created for the
citizens by Cimon in the 460s and dedicated to the god Academos. It was
later to become famous as the site of Plato's school.

1023: This man is unknown and only mentioned here and in Aristophanes'
Acharnians (line 1150), though the scholia insist that it is not the same person.

Presenting such a fine defense
In praise of pride and sound good sense.
What blessed men you once did raise
1030   *Before our time, in olden days.*

        (Addressing the Inferior Argument)

So be creative with your modern art.
This man has made a very good start.

If you want to avoid looking completely foolish and win this
        argument,
1035   then I think you had better use some of your crafty techniques.

INFERIOR:
        In point of fact, I've been standing here for quite some time
        literally busting a gut to confound his ridiculous statements
        with my "counterintelligence." Why else do you think the
        philosophers
        named me the Inferior Argument? Because it was I who created
1040   the concept of disputing entrenched ideals and ethics.
        My dear boy, don't you see? To be able to take up the Inferior
        Argument and win
        is worth far, far more than any number of silver coins you could
        care to count.
        Let's examine these educational methods that he regards with
        such great confidence.
        First of all, I clearly heard him say that he would abolish all
        bathing in warm water
1045   Tell me, sir, if you will, the basis for your belief that hot baths are bad?

SUPERIOR:
        That they are most reprehensible and make the men who take
        them effeminate!

INFERIOR:
        I've got you! You're quite pinned down and there's no escape!
        Now tell me this, which son of Zeus do you believe has the finest
        spirit and had successfully undertaken the most labors?

SUPERIOR:
1050   As far as I am concerned, there is no better man than Heracles.

INFERIOR:

Precisely! And have you ever seen a cold Heraclean bath?
And who could possibly be more manly than Heracles?

SUPERIOR:

That's exactly why the gymnasiums are empty, because the youth
of today are all at the bath houses spouting this kind of claptrap!

INFERIOR:

Next, you take exception to our youngsters frequenting the public
marketplace,   1055
whereas I wholeheartedly recommend it. After all, if meeting in
public is so appalling,
why does Homer describe Nestor and other men of wisdom as
"public speakers"?
Let me now take up the issue of the tongue, which he states is not
seemly for
the young to exercise. I have to disagree, and am of the opposite
opinion.
In addition, he pronounces that one must be discreet, a pair of
fatal assumptions.   1060
I would dearly love for you to tell me anyone who gained the
slightest benefit
from behaving discreetly, just name them and prove me wrong.

SUPERIOR:

There's plenty. What about Peleus, he won a knife for his discretion.

INFERIOR:

A knife! What a delightful little thing to earn, by Zeus.
Even Hyperbolus, who's made a heap of cash swindling us all   1065

1051: According to legend, natural warm springs were a gift from the
craftsman god Hephaestus to Heracles.

1063: Peleus was falsely accused of rape by Hippolyta, the wife of the king
of Iolcus, after he had refused her sexual advances. He was banished to Mt.
Pelion, where he was left at the mercy of wild beasts. The gods took pity
and sent him a knife for protection.

at the lamp market, can't boast that he ever earned a knife!

SUPERIOR:
Thanks to his discretion, Peleus won the right to marry Thetis.

INFERIOR:
Yes, a little too discreet between the sheets, I heard, that's why
she ran out on him, because he simply wasn't outrageous enough
in bed.*

1070   You know some women like it that way, you horny old Cronus stud!
Just consider, dear boy, what a life of discretion consists of,
and all the hedonistic delights you would miss out on—boys, girls,
drinking games, fancy food, fine wine, a good laugh.
How on earth could you endure life without these necessities?

1075   Now, let us move on and discuss the needs of human nature.*
Suppose that you've been indulging in an illicit love affair. You
are discovered!
A scandal! What will you do? You are finished, because you don't
have the means
to argue your way out of trouble. But if you choose to make my
acquaintance,
your nature can run free, with a spring in your step and a smile on
your face,
and shameful thoughts will never even cross your mind. If the

1080   husband accuses you
of adultery, plead innocence and blame Zeus. Say that clearly he
can't resist his lust
for women, so how can you, a mere mortal, be expected to have
more strength than a god?

1066: Aristophanes calls Hyperbolus a "lamp maker" in *Peace* (line 690) and
Knights (line 1315). His family may have once sold lamps in the market.

1067: A beautiful sea-nymph coveted by Zeus and Poseidon. She was
married to the virtuous and mortal Peleus to nullify a prophecy that she
would bear a son more powerful than his father. The son of Peleus and
Thetis was Achilles.

1078: Athenian law acquitted a husband of murder if he caught an
adulterer engaged in sexual relations with his wife.

SUPERIOR:
> Yes, but what if he takes your advice and gets punished by pubic
> plucking, scrotal singeing,
> and a jolly good rectal radish ramming. No argument of yours is
> going to help him after that!

INFERIOR:
> You mean people might think that he was gay?   *1085*

SUPERIOR:
> Yes, what could possibly be worse than that?

INFERIOR:
> Will you concede to me if I can prove this point to you?

SUPERIOR:
> If you can, you'll not hear another peep out of me.

INFERIOR:
> How would you describe most of our lawyers?

SUPERIOR:
> They're gay.   *1090*

INFERIOR:
> Quite right, and what about our tragic dramatists?

SUPERIOR:
> All gay.

INFERIOR:
> Yes, indeed. And our politicians?

SUPERIOR:
> Definitely gay.

1084: Adulterers were left at the mercy of the wronged husband. It seems
that instead of killing the violator, it was more normal to accept a monetary
payment and then inflict a degrading punishment.

1085: The Greek has *eurupróktos*, which means "wide-arse."

INFERIOR:
Then surely you must see that you are defending a lost cause.
1095   I mean, take a good look at the audience,
what would you call most of them?

SUPERIOR:
I'm looking.

INFERIOR:
And what do you see?

SUPERIOR:
By all the gods, most of them are . . . gay!

(He starts pointing at individual members of the audience.)

Well I know he is, and he definitely is,
1100   and that long-haired chap over there and . . . oh my!

INFERIOR:
Well then, what have you got to say for yourself now?

SUPERIOR:
I have to admit that you fuckers
have beaten me.
Here, take my cloak,
I think I might give it a try myself!

(Exit Superior Argument through the stage left door.)

INFERIOR:
(To Strepsiades) Well then, what do you think? Are you and your
1105   son going to run off home,
or are you going to leave the boy with me to learn my oratorical arts?

STREPSIADES:
He's all yours to teach, and you have my permission to beat
him too.
Remember, I want him to have a razor-sharp tongue, and fully
adjustable too, with one edge honed for petty lawsuits and
the other
1110   sharpened for cutting to the chase on more serious matters.

INFERIOR:
Have no fear, he will return an expert in sophistry.

PHEIDIPPIDES:
I'll return a pasty-faced fiend, you mean!

CHORUS:
Go on, off you go.

(Exit Inferior Argument and Pheidippides through the stage left door into the Pondertorium.)

I think that one day you may well
rue the day you did this.

(Exit Strepsiades through the stage right door into his house.)

It's time to tell the judges why we should have first prize,   1115
And why honoring this Cloud chorus will prove extremely wise.
When you're ploughing all your fields and you reach the sowing date,
We'll rain on your land first and make the others wait.
What's more, we'll watch your vines and carefully guard your crops.
We'll stop them getting parched and swamped by huge raindrops.   1120
But if on the other hand you mortals treat us with disrespect
We goddesses will shower you with our malicious effects.
Your lands will yield you nothing, your wine cellars deplete,
For your olives and your grapes will be pelted by our sleet.
When we see you baking bricks and laying tiles of clay,   1125
We'll crack them with our hail, then wash them all away.
Should a friend or family member happen to be wed,
We'll blow a gale all night and keep him from his bed.
You'd rather be in Egypt sizzling in the desert sun,
Than make an unfair judgment and not vote us number one!   1130

(Enter Strepsiades from the stage right door.)

1115: Athenian plays were presented as part of a dramatic competition in honor of the god Dionysus and would have been judged by a panel of referees. The chorus also address the judges in *Birds* (lines 1102–17).

STREPSIADES:

Let's see now; five, four, three, two . . . oh no, only two more days until the old-and-new day at the end of the month, the day I fear the most, the day that makes me tremble, the day that gives me the jitters,

the day that debts are due! Every last one of my creditors will have
1135   paid their court fees and are planning to destroy me, once and for all! They won't listen: I've pleaded with them to give me more time, begged

to have my credit extended, implored them to write off my debts. But nothing works, they all want paying, they just call me a criminal, hurl abuse, and threaten me with the law! The unfeeling bastards!

(He walks toward the stage left door.)

1140   Well, let them try it, that's what I say, they can take me to court for all I care, they'll be sorry, if my Pheidippides has learned how to talk the talk. Well there's only one way to find out, I'll give the Pondertorium a knock and see if he's ready.

(Strepsiades knocks on the door.)

Boy! Boy! Open up! Boy!

(Enter Socrates.)

SOCRATES:
1145   Ah, Strepsiades, good day to you.

STREPSIADES:

Likewise mate! I've brought you a little gift, here.

*(Strepsiades hands Socrates a small bag of barley.)**

It's right and proper to bring a present for the teacher.

1131: Days were counted forward until the twentieth, when, in accordance with the waning of the moon, they ran backward. The final day of the month was called the "old-and-new day" as there was said to be no moon until the first day of the next month.

1135: Due to the transitory nature of the "old-and-new day," it was set aside for the collection of debts, interest, and the placing of court deposits to register proceedings against a debtor.

Has my lad learned the argument, you know, the one
that did that little turn for us a while ago?

SOCRATES:
Indeed he has.

STREPSIADES:
Oh, Mistress of Misrepresentation, how marvelous!   1150

SOCRATES:
Now you will be able to contest all the litigation you please.

STREPSIADES:
What? Even if a witness swore that they saw me borrow the cash?

SOCRATES:
Even if there were a thousand witnesses!

(*Strepsiades breaks into a joyous song.*)

STREPSIADES:
*Then be it known, let my shouts attest**
That all the moneylenders have cause to mourn,   1155
For I banish your debts and compound interest.
I've no more need to endure your scorn.

For today my prodigy has sprung
From within these very walls
Armed with a glinting two-edged tongue   1160
To save my house and foes forestall.

So run and fetch him with a shout,
He will relieve his father's woes.
Call my child, have him come out,   1165
*Come forth my son, it is time to go.**

(*Enter Pheidippides from the stage left door.*)

1150: Strepsiades has already embraced "Basin" (*dinos*) as a god. It seems
only natural that he would now be worshipping this fictitious goddess of
fraud.

SOCRATES:
I believe this is the man you are looking for.

STREPSIADES:
My dear boy! My dear, dear boy!

SOCRATES:
Take him and be on your way.

(Exit Socrates through the stage left door.)

STREPSIADES:
1170   My son! My child!
Hooray! Hooray!
Just let me look at you! What a lovely skin tone!
I can see the contention and the negation written all over your face.
You look like a true Athenian now, with our characteristic "I've no idea
what you're talking about" look blooming in your cheeks. Why, you've even
picked up the look-of-righteous-indignation-even-when-you're-
1175   in-the-wrong expression.
Now you can save me, since it was you who got me into this mess in the first place.

PHEIDIPPIDES:
What are you are so afraid of?

STREPSIADES:
Why, the old-and-new day, of course!

PHEIDIPPIDES:
Are you trying to tell me that there's a day that's both old and new?

STREPSIADES:
Of course there is! It's the day when my creditors will file their
1180   court deposits.

1172: Presumably the actor playing Pheidippides has changed his mask and now resembles the students met at line 133, with a pallid complexion and gaunt features.

PHEIDIPPIDES:
Then, they'll lose their money, won't they? There's no way that one day
can suddenly become two days, is there?

STREPSIADES:
Isn't there?

PHEIDIPPIDES:
Of course not. I mean that's like saying that a single woman could be both
a young girl and an old woman at exactly the same time.

STREPSIADES:
But it's the law. 1185

PHEIDIPPIDES:
No, no, no. They've obviously completely misconstrued the law.

STREPSIADES:
What does the law really mean, then?

PHEIDIPPIDES:
Solon, the elder statesman, was essentially a benefactor of the people, correct?

STREPSIADES:
What's that got to do with the old-and-new day?

PHEIDIPPIDES:
He was the one who decreed that there should be two days
set aside for the issuing of court summonses, and that all deposits 1190
must be lodged on the new day.

STREPSIADES:
Then why did he add the old day too?

1187: Solon was a sixth-century Athenian statesman, lawgiver, and poet. He abolished the practice of placing a free man in slavery for the nonpayment of debts. He was widely regarded as a wise benefactor and founding father of the Athenian state.

PHEIDIPPIDES:
> My dear fellow, to give the accused the opportunity to settle out
> of court
> one day prior to their scheduled trials. Then they would avoid
> harassment
1195 by their creditors until the actual morning of the new day.*

STREPSIADES:
> If that's the case, why do the court officials receive deposits
> on the old *and* new day instead of just on the new day?

PHEIDIPPIDES:
> Isn't it obvious, they're double-dipping.
> They're just like the festival taste-testers*
1200 filching a foretaste of the fees as fast as is feasible!

STREPSIADES:
> Ha ha! You poor fools! You don't stand a chance! Look at you
> simpletons sitting
> out there, just begging to be ripped off by us members of the
> intelligentsia!
> You're dunderheads, clods, and empty vessels, nothing but a herd
> of sheep!
> It is time I serenaded this splendid good fortune
1205 with a nice hymn in honor of me and my son.

> *(Strepsiades breaks into song.)*

> *"O, Strepsiades, you are the lucky one*
> *So fortunate and so wise,*
> *You've raised a fine, upstanding son."*
> *Thus my friends will eulogize.*

1210 *When they find out I have a winner,*
> *You'll see the jealousy on their faces,*
> *So let's celebrate with a great big dinner*
> *Before you argue all my cases.*

1213: It is not known where the creditors enter from, possibly from behind
the *skene* building and onto the stage from stage left. An entrance from the
orchestra wings would have taken too long.

(Exit Strepsiades and Pheidippides through the stage right door. Enter First Creditor and a witness.)

FIRST CREDITOR:
So what's a man supposed to do, throw his own money down the drain?
Not likely, I shouldn't have felt so embarrassed, I should have just said no   1215
right when he asked me for the loan, then I wouldn't be in this mess.*

(Addressing the witness)

And I wouldn't have to waste your time dragging you all the way down here
to witness a summons for money that was rightfully mine in the first place.
Both ways I lose, either my money or the good will of a neighbor.
It's no good worrying about it, I have my duty as a true Athenian,   1220
I must go to court. I hereby summon Strepsiades to appear in . . .

(Enter Strepsiades from the stage right door.)

STREPSIADES:
Who is it?

FIRST CREDITOR:
. . . in court on the old-and-new day.

STREPSIADES:
Did you hear that? He's summoned me on two different days.
Why, pray, are you summoning me?

FIRST CREDITOR:
You owe me twelve hundred drachmas. You borrowed   1225
the money to purchase that dapple-gray horse.

STREPSIADES:
A horse! Did you hear that? Everyone knows that I can't stand horses.

1225: The same amount entered in Strepsiades' ledger as "owed to Pasias" (line 23). The First Creditor may indeed be Pasias in person.

FIRST CREDITOR:
You made a sacred oath before the gods that you would repay me.

STREPSIADES:
Indeed I did, but you see, that was before my lad Pheidippides
had gone and learned the unbeatable Argument.

FIRST CREDITOR:
1230   I see, and I suppose now you think you can simply forgo your debts?

STREPSIADES:
Don't you think it's reasonable that I receive some benefit from his
education?

FIRST CREDITOR:
Well then, if that's the way you want it. Are you willing to refute
your oath before the gods while standing on sacred ground?

STREPSIADES:
Which particular gods?

FIRST CREDITOR:
Zeus, Hermes, and Poseidon.

STREPSIADES:
1235   Of course! I'd even pay three obols for the privilege.

*(The First Creditor is shocked and angry, becoming agitated and
animated.)*

FIRST CREDITOR:
By all the gods! May you be damned for your blasphemy!

*(Strepsiades grabs hold of the First Creditor and pats him on the
belly.)*

STREPSIADES:
You know if we were to split you open and rub you down
with salt, your belly would make a lovely wineskin.

FIRST CREDITOR:
How dare you!

STREPSIADES:
It'd hold at least four jugs' worth.

FIRST CREDITOR:
By Zeus almighty, by all the gods, you'll never get away with this! *1240*

STREPSIADES:
Ha, ha! That's a good one that is, "by all the gods!" Don't make me
laugh!
Those of us "in the know" realize that Zeus is just a joke.

FIRST CREDITOR:
I'm telling you, soon enough, you'll pay for this. Just tell me one
thing,
do you have any intention of paying what you owe me?

STREPSIADES:
Hang on, I'll let you know . . . *1245*

    (Strepsiades runs inside the stage right door.)

FIRST CREDITOR:
(To the witness) What's he up to now? Do you reckon he's going to
pay me?

    (Strepsiades comes out again holding a kneading board.)

STREPSIADES:
Where's that man demanding money? Right then, tell me what
this is.

FIRST CREDITOR:
That? It's a meal-kneader, of course.

STREPSIADES:
And you have the gall to ask me for money! How could you be so
stupid?

1239: This seemingly nonsensical diversion into pure physical comedy may
actually be a comic reference to Strepsiades' abortive attempts to grasp the
concepts of "measures" taught by Socrates (lines 641–45).

1250   You won't catch me parting with a single obol to such a moron.
        You're the one who "needs the fee," it's obviously a "fe-meal
        kneader."

        (Strepsiades tries to dismiss the First Creditor.)

FIRST CREDITOR:
        I take it that you have no intention of paying your debt.

STREPSIADES:
        Not likely, now turn around, get off my doorstep, go on, piss off!

FIRST CREDITOR:
        I will go, straight to the court to lodge my deposit.
1255   I'll see you prosecuted if it's the last thing I do!

        (Exit First Creditor and Witness.)

STREPSIADES:
        You'll just be adding that to those twelve hundred drachmas and
          increasing
        your losses. Will you people never learn?
        I feel sorry for him really, I mean, imagine not knowing your gender!

        (Enter Second Creditor.)

SECOND CREDITOR:
        Oh, no! No!

STREPSIADES:
        Ah!
1260   What now! Who the blazes is this chap, warbling dirges?
        Looks like he's wandered away from a scene in a tragedy.

SECOND CREDITOR:
        Why do you care to know my name? I am doomed, doomed!*

1261: The Greek names Carcinus here, a tragic dramatist who had won first
place at the City Dionysia in 446.

STREPSIADES:
Well go and be doomed somewhere else, will you!

SECOND CREDITOR:
Oh, heartless demons, oh calamity that destroyed my chariot!*
Oh, Pallas Athena, you have brought me rack and ruin!   *1265*

STREPSIADES:
The true tragedy is how you're mutilating those lines.

SECOND CREDITOR:
You may mock me, sir, but all I want is for your son to repay
the money that he borrowed from me, particularly in light
of my recent hapless misadventure.

STREPSIADES:
What money?   *1270*

SECOND CREDITOR:
The money that I lent him.

STREPSIADES:
Oh dear, I can see that you're in a bit of a mess.

SECOND CREDITOR:
I was rounding a bend and fell out of my chariot.

STREPSIADES:
Out of your mind, more like! I think you're the one who's
"round the bend," coming here spouting gibberish.

SECOND CREDITOR:
It is not gibberish, I just want to be repaid!

STREPSIADES:
You're clearly quite insane, a lost cause, I'm afraid.   *1275*

SECOND CREDITOR:
What do you mean?

STREPSIADES:
I believe that you have been knocked senseless, your brain's addled.

SECOND CREDITOR:
  And I believe that I'll be seeing you in court, by Hermes,
  if you don't pay me back the money that I'm owed!

STREPSIADES:
  Tell me something, when Zeus makes it rain, do you believe that
      he sends
  fresh water each time, or that the sun absorbs the moisture from
1280   the earth,
  reclaims it, and sends it back down again in the form of a rain shower?

SECOND CREDITOR:
  I have absolutely no idea, and I don't see what it has to do with . . .

STREPSIADES:
  Well how can you justify reclaiming your money if you
  don't understand the rudiments of meteorology?

SECOND CREDITOR:
1285 Listen, if you can't handle the whole payment this month,
  then how about just paying me the interest?

STREPSIADES:
  What do you mean, "interest"? I'm not in the least bit interested in
  your problems.*

SECOND CREDITOR:
  I mean the charge on the loan that increases in size
  from day to day and month to month as time flows on by.

STREPSIADES:
1290 That's all very well, but do you think the sea
  has increased in size at all since olden times?

SECOND CREDITOR:
  By Zeus, of course not, it would be against
  the law of nature for the sea to change in size.

1281: This parodies the theories of Anaximander, Diogenes, and other
natural philosophers.

STREPSIADES:
Well then, you pitiful wretch, if the sea doesn't increase in size
with all the rivers flowing into it, who the blazes do you think
you are to try and increase the size of your loan! Now bugger off   *1295*
away from my house, or you'll get a damn good prodding!

(Strepsiades calls inside his house.)

Boy! Bring me my cattle prod!

(A slave rushes out of the stage right door with a cattle prod.)

SECOND CREDITOR:
Help! Somebody witness this!

(Strepsiades starts prodding the Second Creditor.)

STREPSIADES:
Giddy up! Get up there! Get going before I brand your horse's arse!

SECOND CREDITOR:
This is outrageous! I protest!

(Strepsiades continues his assault.)

STREPSIADES:
Giddy up! Move it! Or I'll make a gelding out of you!   *1300*

*(The Second Creditor flees offstage, and Strepsiades calls out after
him.)*

Oh, you can move quickly enough when you want to! You can
take your
horses and your chariot wheels and stick them where the sun
don't shine!

(Exit Strepsiades through the stage right door.)

CHORUS:
Depravity often proves a fatal attraction
That can drive an old man to distraction.

1297: The Greek has *kentron* ("goad" or "point"), which has phallic
connotations and is also employed in *Wasps* (lines 225, 408, 115).

1305   *This one thinks he can evade his debts,*
       So he'll push his luck and hedge his bets.
       But we all know that one day soon,
       There will come an end to this honeymoon,
       That will force our sophist roughly back
1310   *From his latest wicked track.*

       For he will discover presently
       The consequences of his desperate plea.
       For his son has learned the wily art
1315   *Of successfully arguing the unjust part.*
       He defeats all opponents however strong
       Even when his case is plainly wrong.
       But I have a feeling that these disputes
1320   *Will make him wish that his son was mute!*

       (Enter a disheveled Strepsiades running out of the stage right
       door.)

STREPSIADES:
   Oh! Oh!
   Help me! Friends, relatives, citizens, help!
   Come quickly! I'm in terrible danger! Please!
   I'm under attack, he's pummeling my head,
   gashing my cheeks! Help me! Help me!

       (Enter Pheidippides from the stage right door, looking very smug.)

1325   You monster! You would dare to strike your own father?*

PHEIDIPPIDES:
   That's right, old man.

STREPSIADES:
   You hear that? He even admits to it!

PHEIDIPPIDES:
   Freely.

STREPSIADES:
   You're despicable, a father beater and a criminal!

PHEIDIPPIDES:
Oh, say those things again, more, more.
You know how I just love to be insulted.

STREPSIADES:
You filthy arsehole! 1330

PHEIDIPPIDES:
Please, keep showering me with roses.

STREPSIADES:
You would dare to raise a hand against your own father?

PHEIDIPPIDES:
Of course I would by Zeus, and moreover I was perfectly
justified in giving you a beating, as well.

STREPSIADES:
You little bugger! How can striking your own father ever be right?

PHEIDIPPIDES:
I'll prove it to you, by arguing my view, and I'll win too.

STREPSIADES:
You'll never win on this point. It's impossible! 1335

PHEIDIPPIDES:
On the contrary, it'll be a walkover. So, decide
which of the two Arguments you want to present.

STREPSIADES:
Which two Arguments?

PHEIDIPPIDES:
The Superior or Inferior.

STREPSIADES:
It's unbellevable, and to think it was I who had you
educated to argue successfully against Justice.
But there's absolutely no way that you're going to be able 1340
to convince me that it is right for a son to beat his own father.

PHEIDIPPIDES:

    Oh, but I shall convince you. In fact, you'll be so convinced once you've heard

    me out, that you'll have nothing at all worthwhile to say on the matter.

STREPSIADES:

    Go on then, let's hear what you have to say for yourself, I can't wait.

CHORUS:

1345   *Old man, it's time you started thinking*
    About what you need to say to win,
    He would not be quite so arrogant
    If he did not have an argument.
    So be aware of his self-assurance,
1350   *It is the reason for his insolence.*

CHORUS:

    Please tell the chorus how you came to be involved in this dispute.
    Tell us in your own words what actually happened.

STREPSIADES:

    Oh, I'll tell you all right, you'll hear every sordid detail of this horrible squabble.

    We were inside enjoying a nice dinner when I asked him to fetch his lyre

    and sing us an after dinner song. I suggested he do a bit of "Hark
1355   the Hallowed Ram

    Was Shorn" by Simonides, but he would have none of it. No, he told me that strumming

    a lyre and singing at dinner parties was "terribly passé" and said that only old women

    grinding barley at the stone sing those kinds of songs anymore!*

PHEIDIPPIDES:

    Yes, and that explains why you received a thrashing. Who do you think you are,

---

1356: Simonides (c.556–468) was a prolific poet who created choral lyrics, dithyrambs, laments, and victory songs.

ordering me to croon some monotonous old song like a chirping
grasshopper? 1360

STREPSIADES:
That's exactly the kind of talk he was spouting inside, and what's
more,
he even had the gall to announce that Simonides was a terrible poet!
I just couldn't believe my ears. Well, I swallowed my anger, for the
moment,
and asked him ever so nicely to pick up the myrtle bough and
recite a little
Aeschylus for me, and do you know what he said! "Oh yes,
Aeschylus, surely 1365
the foremost of all poets at being loud, pompous, bombastic, and
inaccessible."
Well, I nearly had a heart attack I was so angry at him, but yet
again, I curbed
my fury and said calmly, "Why don't you come up with some of
that clever
modern stuff, something from one of those fashionable poets
you're always
going on about." And with that he blurted out some disgusting
lines from Euripides, 1370
about a brother and sister going at it together! Well, that was it,
the last straw,
I could contain myself no longer, and I let him have it, I told him
just what I thought and it wasn't pretty either, what's more he
answered
me back with some of the foulest language I have ever heard. At
that moment
he leapt to his feet and weighed into me, first pushing and
shoving, then he grabbed 1375
my throat and started shaking me and punching and kicking. It
was terrible!

1365: Aeschylus (525/4–456/5) was one of the most famous and respected
Athenian tragedians.

1370: This tragic dramatist (485/4?–407/6) was a contemporary of
Aristophanes. This could be a reference to Euripides' *Aeolus* (fr. 14–41), the
brother being Macareus and the sister Canace.

PHEIDIPPIDES:
> I was well within my rights to punish you, after you dared to
> insult a gifted man like Euripides.

STREPSIADES:
> Gifted! He's just a . . . No, you'll only lay into me all over again.

PHEIDIPPIDES:
> And I'd be justified too, by Zeus!

STREPSIADES:
> How would you be justified? You insolent ruffian, have you
> 1380   forgotten who raised you?
> I was the one who had to listen to your lisping baby talk, when
> you went "wu-wu!"
> I knew what you wanted and would fetch you something to
> drink. Then you would go
> "foo-foo!" and daddy here would get you some bread. And when
> you cried "poo-poo!"
> it was me who would pick you up, take you outside, and let you
> 1385   do your little doo-doos!
> But you, on the other hand, couldn't care less about my needs.
> Why just then, when you
> were strangling me, I was completely ignored, even though I was
> screaming that I was
> about to shit my pants, you just kept right on throttling away. You
> literally squeezed
> the crap out of me, and I did my poo-poo right there and then!
> 1390   It's a disgraceful way to treat your dear old dad.

CHORUS:
> *The hearts of the young are all a flutter*
> *To hear what words this lad might utter*
> *To justify such disrespect*
> *Could ever be deemed correct*
> 1395   *For such an outcome would surely mean*
> *That an old man's hide's not worth a bean!*

CHORUS:
> Now, you mover and shaker, you maestro of modernity, it is your turn.
> You must persuade him to accept your point of view.

PHEIDIPPIDES:

Let me first say how pleasurable it is to be acquainted with
modern ways and intelligent
notions, for it enables one to disdain conventional practices from a
superior vantage point. 1400
When I filled my brain with only the mindless thoughts of horse
riding I could hardly even blurt
out three words without making some stupid mistake. But thanks
to my adversary here,
who saw to my education, I now possess a keen intellect and am
proficient in finite conception,
subtle argument, and detailed contemplation. In effect, I believe
that I have the necessary skills
to fully demonstrate that it is perfectly justified to discipline one's
own father. 1405

STREPSIADES:

I wish you'd go back to your horses, by Zeus! I would much
rather have to pay
for a four-horse chariot team than run the risk of sustaining bodily
harm every day!

PHEIDIPPIDES:

If I may be allowed to return to the point in my argument from
where I was so rudely
interrupted. Tell me this, did you ever have occasion to beat me
when I was a child?

STREPSIADES:

Yes, but it was always for your own good. I had your best interests
at heart. 1410

PHEIDIPPIDES:

Then surely it is justified for me to beat you for your own good, if,
by your definition,
"having someone else's best interests at heart" means to beat
them? How is it justified
that your body should be protected against beatings but mine
not? Is it not true that we

are both free men? "Suffer the little children, do you think the
father should not?"
No doubt you will attempt to defend yourself by stating that it is

1415   quite legitimate for
this kind of punishment to be meted out to children, and yet, I
would say that the
elderly are living a "second childhood." This being the case,
surely it is only right
that the elderly should be chastised more severely than the young,
as they should
have certainly learned right and wrong after a lifetime of experience.

STREPSIADES:
There's not a place in the world where it is legitimate for a son to

1420   beat his father!

PHEIDIPPIDES:
But it is men who make legislation, men just like you and me. In
past times,
one man simply persuaded another that this was the way things
should be.*
Therefore what is preventing me from similarly stating a new
"law" for times to come
specifying that sons should be permitted to beat their fathers in
return?
"This will not be retroactive legislation, and all claims for

1425   compensation for blows
previously sustained will not be considered and shall hereby be
stricken from the record."
Examine chickens and other such farmyard animals, you will see
that they freely
attack their fathers, and how are they so very different from us?
Except, of course, that they refrain from drafting statutes.

1414: This is a parody of a line from Euripides' *Alcestis* (691) originally
produced in 438 (**1414 *Alcestis***).

1426: A lampoon on the legal language found in contemporary Athenian
decrees.

1428: See *Birds* lines 1349–50.

STREPSIADES:
  If you're so keen to take after farmyard fowl, why don't you start   1430
  eating chicken shit and roosting on a perch in the hen house?

PHEIDIPPIDES:
  Sir, your analogy is hardly relevant, and I am sure Socrates would
  agree with me.

STREPSIADES:
  Then stop hitting me, otherwise you'll come to regret it.

PHEIDIPPIDES:
  And why would that be?

STREPSIADES:
  Well, when you have a son of your own,   1435
  you'll not have the right to beat him, as I did you!

PHEIDIPPIDES:
  But what if I don't have a son, then I would have suffered
  for nothing, and you'll be laughing at me from beyond the grave.

  (Strepsiades addresses the audience.)

STREPSIADES:
  You know what, friends, he does have a point, and it seems
  only proper that we give the young the benefit of the doubt now
    and again.
  I suppose it's only reasonable that we should suffer a little if we
  step out of line.

PHEIDIPPIDES:
  And another thing . . .   1440

STREPSIADES:
  No! I can't take it any more!

PHEIDIPPIDES:
  Just listen, perhaps it will make your suffering seem not so bad.

STREPSIADES:
What are you talking about? Nothing could comfort my pain.

PHEIDIPPIDES:
I shall beat Mother just as I beat you.

STREPSIADES:
WHAT! What are you saying? This is going from bad to worse!

PHEIDIPPIDES:
1445   But I can use the inferior argument to defeat you on this very subject.
I can prove that it is right to beat one's mother.

STREPSIADES:
And what then?
What then? I ask you!
You're all doomed!
1450   You're going to throw yourself into the abyss.
You, Socrates, and that damned Inferior Argument!

(Strepsiades looks up and calls out.)

Clouds! This is all your fault, you're responsible!
I trusted you, I believed in you!

CHORUS:
You brought this trouble on yourself when you took
1455   the twisting path of wickedness and deceit.

STREPSIADES:
But why didn't you tell me that in the first place?
I'm just a simple old yokel. You lured me into this mess!

CHORUS:
But we always do this.
When we discover a mortal who becomes
1460   enamored by vice, we drive them to despair.
That is how we teach man to have proper respect for the gods.

STREPSIADES:
Oh, Clouds, you've treated me harshly, but you're right,

I should never have tried to get of out paying my debts.

(To Pheidippides)

Come on, my lad, let's get even with Socrates and Chaerephon,
those villains, it's high time they met their makers!   *1465*
Let's pay them back for the vile way they deceived us.

PHEIDIPPIDES:
But I must not offend my teachers.

STREPSIADES:
Yes, yes, and "we venerate Zeus protector of fathers."

PHEIDIPPIDES:
Just listen to you, "father Zeus." You're so old fashioned!
Zeus doesn't exist.   *1470*

STREPSIADES:
Yes he does.

PHEIDIPPIDES:
No he doesn't. "Zeus has been overthrown, Basin is king now."

STREPSIADES:
He hasn't been overthrown, I was misled by this basin.

*(Indicating the wine basin set on a stand outside the
Pondertorium)*

Oh, what a stupid wretch I am, to believe that a piece
of clay pottery could ever be a god!

PHEIDIPPIDES:
I've had enough of you. You can rant and rave to yourself. I'm not
listening!   *1475*

1469: This is more than likely an unknown quote from a tragedy referring
to Zeus Patroos, the protector and patron god of fathers.

(Exit Pheidippides into the house, through the stage right door.)

STREPSIADES:
 Oh, I must have been completely out of my mind,
 to think I rejected the gods because Socrates told me to.
 Unbelievable! What was I thinking? Dear, dear Hermes,*
 take pity on me, please be kind, don't destroy me now.
1480 I know I behaved like a raving maniac, but it was all because of them
 and their philosophical drivel. I need you now, help me, tell me
  what
 can I do to redeem myself? Should I file a lawsuit against them?
 What? What can I do?

(Strepsiades suddenly realizes what he must do.)

       Yes, that's it, that's exactly right,
 I'm not going to fiddle around with lawsuits, no, I'll burn
1485 those babbling bastards out, that's what I'll do! Xanthias! Xanthias!
 Come here at once and bring the ladder and an axe!

*(A slave comes running out of the stage right door with a ladder
and an axe. He lays the ladder on the skene building.)*

 I want you to climb up onto the roof of the Pondertorium
 and do a hatchet job on their roof, and if you care anything
 for your poor old master, you'll really bring the house down
1490 on those charlatans. Light up a torch and hand it to me!*

(Xanthias hands him a flaming torch.)

 Now it's my turn to call in the debts, those colossal cheats
 are going to pay dearly for what they put me through!

*(Strepsiades and Xanthias climb up onto the roof of the skene
building.)**

STUDENT:
 Oh! Oh!

STREPSIADES:
 "Come torch, send on your mighty blaze!"

(Enter a student from the stage left door hatch, who sees Strepsiades on the roof.)

STUDENT 1:
You there! What are you up to?   *1495*

STREPSIADES:
I'm demonstrating to your rafters the finer points of my axe!

(Enter another student from the window.)*

STUDENT 2:
Ahhh! Who set our house on fire?

STREPSIADES:
You should know, you thieves, you lot stole his cloak!

STUDENT 1:
You'll kill us all! Kill us all!

STREPSIADES:
Well at least you're right about that, as long as I don't   *1500*
get carried away with my axe and come a cropper!

(Enter Socrates from the window.)

SOCRATES:
You up there, whatever do you think you are doing?

STREPSIADES:
I am "walking the air to look down on the sun!"

(Enter Chaerephon from the stage left door.)

CHAEREPHON:
Ahhh! Help! I'm suffocating!

SOCRATES:
What about me? I'm going up in smoke!   *1505*

STREPSIADES:

It serves you right for daring to think that you could snub the gods
and spy on the moon when she's all exposed. Outrageous!
Chase then down, smash bash and crash them! We'll teach them
a hundred lessons, but most of all never to offend the gods above!

(Exit Strepsiades and Xanthias into the Pondertorium.)

CHORUS:

1510   *And now it's time we closed this play*
         We've performed enough for you today!

(Exit the chorus rapidly offstage.)

—END—

Endnotes

Stage Direction: Strepsiades. The name means "son of Twister" and becomes appropriate through the course of the play as Strepsiades attempts to "twist" his way out of his debts. For the meaning of "Pheidippides" see the note on line 66.

Stage Direction: Asleep. Strepsiades and his son may be lying on the *ekkyklema*—the moveable platform that either revolved or was trucked from the central doorway. If this was the case, it could have been withdrawn at some point during the opening scene once both characters were awake.

8: Enemy territory. Shortly after the original production of *Clouds* in March of 423 B.C.E., Athens and Sparta settled on a one-year truce. One of the terms was that neither party should receive deserters. Previously, runaway slaves had been granted immunity if they reached enemy territory.

24: Taken for a ride. The Greek has "the horse with the *koppa* brand." Koppa was an old letter of the Greek alphabet that had fallen out of use by the fifth century but could still be found as a brand mark for livestock. Aristophanes creates a pun on *koppa* and *koptein* (to strike/knock) with the next line, which reads, "I would rather have knocked my eye out with a stone."

38: Bed bailiffs. The Greek names the Demarch, the highest elected official presiding over one of the 139 demes, the small administrative areas that formed Attica. The deme had its own assembly and local government and the Demarch was responsible in administering the collection of debts.

48: Little lady. The Greek has "all Coesyrated," a reference to Cocsyra,

101

another prominent member of the Alcmaeonid clan. She is named as an aristocrat in Aristophanes' *Acharnians* (line 614).

52: Aphrodite all over and everywhere Eros. The Greek has "All Colias and Genetyllis." Colias was a promontory near Phaleron where a sanctuary of Aphrodite, the goddess of love, was located. There is also a pun on *Kôlias* (Colias) and *kôlê* (penis). Genetyllis was a sacred spirit associated with Aphrodite and lovemaking.

55: Whacking it. A sexual double entendre for excessive sexual intercourse, extravagance, and the wasting of wealth (Henderson 1991, pp. 171–72).

70: Drive a chariot. Such a scene is depicted on the Parthenon frieze (South frieze slab XXX, Boardman *GS2*, fig. 96.7). Pindar celebrated the victory of Megacles in a chariot race at Delphi held in 486 in his Seventh Pythian Ode.

83: God of horses. As well as being the god of the sea and the "earth shaker," Poseidon was known as "Hippios," the god of horses. This cult was quite widespread in Greece, and he was often depicted with horses or riding a chariot. In myth Poseidon is often credited with fathering the horse (Burkert 1985, pp. 136–39).

98: Casserole dish. The Greek has "baking cover," a clay covering used to bake bread and heated by stacking hot coals around it. The comic playwright Cratinus attributed this analogy of the universe to the philosopher Hippon (fr. 155). It is also found in *Birds* lines 1000–1. (For a pictorial representation of a baking cover see Sparkes and Talbot, figs. 36 and 37.)

103: Barefoot. In Plato's *Symposium* (220b) Alcibiades tells how Socrates went barefoot even in the bitter cold of Thrace when they served together during the Potidaea campaign in 431. Also in the *Symposium* (174a) Apollodorus tells of how he saw Socrates wearing sandals and describes this as "an unusual event." Socrates explained that he was going out to dinner and wanted to look his best.

104: Chaerephon. He was lampooned for his pallid, sickly appearance, which earned him the nickname of "the living dead" or "the bat" (*Birds* lines 1296 and 1564). No written works by Chaerephon have survived, but he is famous for asking the oracle at Delphi if there was anyone wiser than Socrates (Plato *Apology* 21a). He died shortly before the trial of Socrates in 399. He also appears as a witness in *Wasps* (line 1408).

113-14: Superior and Inferior Arguments. The origin of this notion may be the sophist Protagoras (490–420), who authored a treatise called

"Controversial Argument" that set out how to turn the weaker argument into a strong and winning defense. Protagoras was credited with being the first philosopher to charge fees for teaching rhetoric, taking advantage of the new Athenian democratic institutions where political dominance was secured by the mastering of oratorical skills. This new command of public speaking taught by the sophists had caused a sensation in the assembly in 427 when Gorgias of Leontini (483–376) delivered a speech championing his city's cause against Syracuse. His use of new oratorical techniques stunned the Athenian citizens and enabled him to remain in Athens teaching these methods. According to Plato, Socrates refuted these very lines and used them as an example of the falsehoods spoken about him by the Athenians (*Apology* 18b and 19b).

145: One flea foot. The close attention paid to the movements of a flea lampoons the sophists and in particular, Socrates' methodology whereby concepts and notions would be expounded, questioned, and analyzed in minute detail. (See lines 740–42.) Socrates himself admitted that his methods were often misinterpreted, and this led to a degree of confusion and hostility (Plato *Apology* 23a).

151: Booties. The Greek has simply "Persians," a type of soft boot worn by women (see Brooke, pp. 73–74).

174: Speckled gecko. In Plato's *Symposium* (220d), Alcibiades tells how Socrates would spend hours standing in one spot considering a problem. In this particular instance, while on active military duty in Potidaea, he stayed in one place all day and all the following night, much to the amusement of his fellow soldiers who camped out to watch him. Likewise, the philosopher Thales was said to have been so preoccupied with gazing up at the sky that he fell down a well and killed himself (Plato *Theaetetus* 174a). The relevance of the gecko joke was unearthed by Carl Anderson in *Classical Philology* 93.1 (1998): 49.

179: Wrestling school. In Plato's *Symposium* (217c) Alcibiades describes how as a young man, he would encourage Socrates to visit him at the gymnasium. See Plato's *Lysias* (203a) for an account of Socrates visiting the wrestling schools.

186: Walking wounded. The Greek has "Spartans we captured at Pylos, after spending a year in our jails." An Athenian force under the command of Cleon and Demosthenes had defeated the Spartans stationed at Sphacteria, near Pylos, two years earlier in 425. The Athenians refused all representations to free them, stating that they would be held until a peace agreement was reached, or killed if Attica was invaded (Thucydides 4.37–41).

188: What lies beneath. This was one of the charges brought against Socrates at his trial. "Socrates is guilty of criminal meddling, in that he inquires into things below the earth and in the sky" (Plato *Apology* 18b).

201: Astronomy. Socrates himself did not seem to hold astronomy in particularly high regard (Plato *Republic* 527d), although there were notable contemporary practitioners in Athens who were linked to the Sophistic movement such as Hippias of Elis and Diogenes of Apollonia.

203: Landlords. The Greek has "cleruchs." These were landlords who had confiscated land allotted to them by the state. In 427 the Athenians successfully put down the revolt of Mytilene (in modern day Lesbos). The land was confiscated and distributed by lot to Athenian citizens who became absentee landlords, receiving rent from the remaining locals (Thucydides 3.50).

Stage Direction: Enter Socrates. Socrates appears suspended over the stage by means of the *machina* (stage crane). He is seated on a board slung at each end by ropes that look like a rack used to dry fruit and vegetables.

223: Ephemeral. The Greek term *ephêmeros* means "a life worth but a day." The same term is found at *Birds* line 687 and Plato's *Laws* 11.923a.

225: Look down on the sun. To most Greeks the sun was Helios, a god, and not a natural element. Socrates is reported by Plato (*Apology* 19c) to have referred to this scene at his trial where he describes his portrayal in "that Aristophanes play where Socrates was shown whirling about announcing that he is walking in the air and all sorts of other nonsense that I know nothing about."

236: A good brainwashing. The Greek has Socrates comparing the effects of the earth on his mind to the growth of watercress. Strepsiades responds, "So thought draws moisture to watercress?"

246: Pay you. Several notable sophists were paid substantial fees for their educational services. In Plato's *Apology* (20a), Socrates denies ever charging a fee for teaching and names Gorgias of Leontini, Prodicus of Ceos, Hippias of Elis, and Callias of Paros (who, according to Socrates, was paid more than the other three combined) as all having received payment for teaching. Socrates does not condemn this practice but makes it clear that the assumption that he made money from his pursuits is false.

249: Byzantine. The Greek has "Do you use those iron bars from Byzantium?" This was a Greek colony on the site of modern day Istanbul, and it used large, heavy iron bars as currency. Iron bars were also thrown into the sea to seal oaths. This form of coinage was common in many Greek states in the archaic period. The Spartans also used such currency, apparently to discourage the accumulation of wealth (Plutarch *Lycurgus* 9). Interestingly Plutarch comments that due to the worthlessness of this iron currency, imports to Sparta were virtually halted, and therefore "no instructor of rhetoric ever set foot on Spartan soil."

257: Make a meal out of me. The Greek has "make an Athamas out of me." Athamas was a legendary Boeotian king who married Nephele ("Cloud"). He had two children by Nephele, Phrixus and Helle, and went on to marry Ino, who became jealous of her semidivine stepchildren. Ino devised a false prophecy which demanded their deaths to curb a famine. Nephele saved her children by means of flying them off on a golden ram. Helle fell into the sea, giving her name to the Hellespont, but Phrixus was taken to safety in Colchis. Athamas was then offered for sacrifice in their place and in some versions rescued by Heracles. Sophocles had presented two tragedies named *Athamas*; one apparently contained a scene depicting Athamas standing by the altar of Zeus, wreathed for sacrifice. Walter Burkert (1983, pp. 114–115) finds a link between the Athamas story and weather magic, which would help explain the relevance of this reference in foreshadowing Socrates' notions of weather, clouds, and Zeus.

260: Rattling castanet. The same term is used of Odysseus' speaking skills in Euripides' *Cyclops* (line 104).

262: A good dusting. The fine flour that "baptizes" Strepsiades is both a parody of initiation rites (new members of the Orphic cult were sprinkled with chalk) and a further joke on the finite nature of sophistic inquiry.

292: Thunderclaps. The theatre at this time may have been equipped with a thunder machine which was used at this point. The use of such a machine called a *bronteion* is suggested by the scholia. However, the style and tone of the choral song could well have created a similar effect (Dover 1968, note on 292).

300: Cecrops. He was sometimes depicted as half man/half serpent, an allusion to his origins from the land (see *Wasps* lines 437–40). Athens was known as the land of Cecrops, and the audience gathered in the Theatre of Dionysus to watch *Clouds* were seated on the southeastern slope of Cecrops' rock, more commonly known as the Acropolis.

325: Left and right. The Greek has "coming from the sides," a reference to the actual entrance of the Cloud-chorus from the *eisodoi* (wings) to the left and right. Aristophanes uses this as a pun in *Birds* (lines 195–96) at the entrance of the chorus.

331–34: Sophisticated scholars. In the Greek the list starts with "Prophets from Thurii." Thurii was an Athenian colony founded in 444/3 in south Italy near the city of Sybaris. The "prophet" probably refers to Lampon, who was in charge of settling the colony. The "atmospheric therapists" may be a reference to Hippocrates of Cos for whom the Hippocratic oath is named. He was certainly a contemporary of Socrates, and some of his medical theories seem to have been based on those of Diogenes of Apollonia. Atmospheric conditions and the nature of the air were regarded by many medical practitioners at this time as having an effect upon the health of the body (Plato *Symposium* 188a-b). For "long-haired loungers, etc.," the Greek has *sphragidonuchargokomêtas*, an Aristophanic creation meaning something like "long-haired-lazy-signet-ring-wearers." These kinds of convoluted comic coinages are often found in Aristophanes such as "Cloudcuckooland" (*Birds* line 819) . The term used here either applies to the well-to-do young gentlemen who sought instruction from the sophists or is a reference to long fingernails, implying the general unkempt state of the men being described. The list concludes with a comic description of dithyrambic poets, composers of choral songs in honor of Dionysus that were often accompanied by a circling or spiraling dance. The traditional construction of the dithyramb was by a system of cyclical strophic responsion. Aristophanes uses similar "airy" terms for his portrayal of the dithyrambic poet Cinesias in *Birds* (lines 1372–1409).

351: Simon. The name Simon is found only in Comedy. A fragment from Eupolis' *Cities* (fr. 218) names him in the context of embezzlement.

362-63: The way you strut. In Plato's *Symposium* (221b) Alcibiades refers to these lines from *Clouds* as being an accurate description of Socrates' behavior during the Athenian forces' withdrawal from Delium in 424.

378: Necessity. *Anankê* was an important element in pre-Socratic theories and can be found in the works of Parmenides, Empedocles, Leucippus, and Democritus. *Anankê* was also a powerful force in tragedy: Aeschylus told of Agamemnon "strapping himself to the yoke of Necessity" when compelled to sacrifice his daughter (*Agamemnon* line 218).

380: Celestial Basin. The *dinos* or mixing bowl was a large basin that stood on a stand (see Boardman *ABFV*, fig. 187, for a pictorial representation). The *dinos* took a central position in the organization and proceedings of the symposium. This was a drinking party frequented by the Athenian intelligentsia, where Socrates and his contemporaries were depicted as meeting and engaging in intellectual discourse (Plato's *Symposium*). *Dinos* also meant "spin" or "whirl," the word being applied to the basin because of its function for mixing wine (the heavy Greek wine was diluted with water). The term is used by Plato (*Phaedo* 99b) to describe how the earth stays in place beneath the heavens. *Dinos* was also used in a similar descriptive context by Empedocles and Democritus. Hence the joke works three ways in *Clouds*:

(1) As a philosopher's term for a natural phenomenon: "the whirling of the celestial *dinos* (vortex)" (line 380).

(2) As a joke on the drinking habits of the sophists: "*Dinos* (wine basin) is king now!" (line 828).

(3) As a household object used as an religious idol (lines 1472–74).

For another view of the role of the *dinos* see Bowie 1997.

407: Spontaneous flame. Both Anaximander and Anaximenes speculated that thunder and lightning were caused by the force of the wind blasting out of thick clouds. Anaxagoras, followed by Democritus, advanced the theory that it was friction that created lightning bolts.

508: Trophonius. The terrifying aspect of entering the shrine of Trophonius was the descent where the initiate plunged through a small aperture, propelled by the suction of a mystical wind (also described by Pausanias as *dinos*). Mention of Trophonius is doubly apt. He was said to have been swallowed by the earth after a botched attempt to steal from one of the Delphic treasuries, and his rites were also connected with issues of memory, forgetfulness, and knowledge. The whole process is vividly described by Pausanias (9.39.5–14), and referred to in Euripides' *Ion* (line 300).

539–40: Cheap laughs from the children. Children in the audience are referred to in Aristophanes' *Peace* (line 50) and *Ecclesiazusae* (line 1146). However, it is not known if children where actually in attendance at the theatre or if these remarks were aimed at the "childish" members of the audience. The costuming of *Clouds* would have almost certainly included a phallus, but Aristophanes may be alluding to a more grotesque type of appendage preferred by other "cruder" comics. He may be simply poking fun at his own conventions as many of the elements he refutes here actually occur in the course of the play.

541: Bald men. Aristophanes himself seems to have been bald (*Knights* lines 550, *Peace* lines 767–73), and Socrates may have been portrayed as a bald or balding character (he would have been in his forties when *Clouds* was staged). Alcibiades in the *Symposium* refers to Socrates as resembling the satyrs Silenus and Marsyas, both of whom are regularly portrayed as balding characters (for images of balding satyrs see Trendall and Webster, figs. 11, 7–10). It is also not unreasonable to presume that Strepsiades himself would have been presented in a bald mask to mark his advanced years.

543–45: Oh! Oh! *Clouds* opens with the cry *iou! iou!* (oh! oh!). Strepsiades calls it out again at line 1321 when attacked by his son, and a student makes the same cry being hotly pursued by Strepsiades carrying flaming torches.

554: A disgusting imitation. Ian Storey has found thirteen close resemblances between the structure and content of *Knights* and the surviving fragments of *Maricas* (Storey in Sommerstein et al., 1993, pp. 383–84). Eupolis' *Maricas* featured a foreign streetwise slave who represented Hyperbolus just as Aristophanes' Paphlagonian slave represented Cleon in *Knights*.

584: "Such sheets of fire." Originally a quote from Sophocles' *Teucer* (fr. 578), "Amid the lightning came the rolling thunder."

617–19: Lunar cycle. Each Greek city-state utilized its own dating system although they were all based on the lunar cycle. In Athens there were twelve months, each named after a festival. The year started with the first new moon after the summer solstice, and each subsequent month was marked by the falling of the old moon, indicating the end of one month, and the rising of the new moon, indicating the beginning of another. Therefore, Athenian months lasted twenty-nine or thirty days. The last day of the month was called the "old-and-new day." It seems that Athenian officials could adjust the calendar to suit particular civic needs such as the postponement or rescheduling of festivals, therefore causing the calendar to fall out of synchronization with the moon (Burkert 1985, 225–6).

632–33: Into the light. Socrates' language is still that of initiation rites. Strepsiades emerges into the light from the secret interior of the Pondertorium. After leaving the cave of Trophonius (see *508 Trophonius), the knowledge seeker was sat on the "throne of remembrance" and questioned by the priests on the nature of what he had learned (Pausanias 9.39.13). The actions of Socrates and the references to Strepsiades' memory, or lack thereof, closely resemble these rites.

651: With your fingers. The Greek has *kata daktulon,* which means "by the fingers." At some point this became a technical term for the measurement of rhythm. Strepsiades misunderstands and either makes a masturbation joke or gives Socrates "the finger" by way of a commonly understood obscene gesture.

659: Correct gender. This is very close to Plato's *Euthydemus* (277e); "First of all, as Prodicus says, you must learn the correct use of words." Both

Prodicus and Protagoras were concerned with the "correct" usage of words and categorized them according to gender (Plato *Cratylus* 391c, Aristotle *Rhetoric* 3.5–1407b).

671: Meal-kneader. For a pictorial representation of a *cardopus* see B. A. Sparkes 1962, p. 126 and Plates IV 4, VII 3 & 4. A *cardopus* is also mentioned in Plato's *Phaedo* (99b) as being used to describe the earth as a flat board or trough supported on a cushion of air.

676: By the back door. The Greek has "He kneads his dough in a round pestle." Dover takes this to mean that Cleonymus is so cowardly that he is forced to masturbate for sexual pleasure (Dover 1989, p. 139). Henderson sees an allusion to anal intercourse, focusing the joke on Cleonymus' "womanly" aspects (Henderson 1991, p. 200) This is closer to the sense of the scene, which lampoons the sophist's concerns with the correct use of gender in grammar.

766. The healers. The Greek *pharmakon* ("healer") is also the term used for the Thessalian witch at line 749. Healing, magic, and sorcery were all closely connected. Glass was a rare and expensive commodity at this time.

845: Legally incompetent. Plato describes a court action whereby the head of a family could be judged to be of "unsound" mind and responsibility for all property be handed to the next of kin (*Laws* 929 d and e) . Xenophon states that Socrates was accused of encouraging the young to use this law against their fathers and then goes on to say that Socrates was adamantly opposed to such action (*Memorabilia* 1.2.49).

862: Festival. This was the Diasia, a family festival where gifts were exchanged. This reference to Pheidippides being given a cart at an early age shows his fascination with chariots beginning in childhood. Such a scene is depicted on an Attic red figure Aryballus with a group of boys playing with toy chariots (Boardman *ARFV1*, fig. 318.2).

870: Grasp your own tackle. A much debated pun based around the Greek *tribôn* ("well worn" or "well known") and *kremasta* ("tackle" or "hanging ropes"). *Tribein* (to rub/chafe) has sexual connotations as a byword for masturbation (Henderson 1991, p. 176 and Aristophanes' *Wasps* line 1344) which is fully exploited in the character of the Triballion ("Jerkoffalot") in *Birds* (lines 1565–1684). *Kremasta* is used of Socrates hanging in the air at line 218. Rope is also used in a sexual sense at *Wasps* (lines 1342–44). Hence Pheidippides turns Socrates' innocent remark into a rude retort.

876: A talent. Prodicus was said to charge fifty drachmas for a course in the correct use of words, only one twelfth of a talent. There is no evidence that

Socrates ever taught Hyperbolus or even charged fees, something he denies vigorously in Plato's *Apology* (19e). This joke seems squarely aimed at Hyperbolus who was frequently lampooned for his lowly origins. The huge sum of money demanded for his training is a comic indication of the amount of work it took to turn him into a presentable orator.

Stage Direction: Enter the Superior Argument. It is not known how the two Arguments were costumed. The scholia state that they are made to resemble a pair of fighting cocks, but there is no reference in the text to this. Costume that represented each character's generation would be appropriate. It may have been that the actor who played Socrates also played the Inferior Argument after a quick mask and costume change.

905: Locking up his father. The position of the father in the Attic household was held to be supreme; therefore offenses by a child against his father were considered to be a very serious breach of moral code. Zeus overthrew his own father, Cronus, to gain the supremacy of heaven, and he chained him up beneath the earth (Hesiod *Theogony* 73). In Aeschylus' *The Furies*, the Furies use this same argument against Apollo and Orestes: "You say that Zeus has higher regard for a father's fate / and yet he placed his own father, Cronus, in chains" (lines 640–41).

908: Queer. The Greek term *katapugôn*, a derivation of *pugê* (arse), was used to describe passive homosexuals. However, it seems that it can also be used as a general term of abuse (Henderson 1991, p. 210), and could also be applied to women (Dover 1989, p. 143).

922: King of the scroungers. The Greek has "Telephus the Mysian." *Telephus* was a tragedy staged by Euripides in 438. The central character was the king of Mysia, an area in the northwest of Asia Minor (modern day Turkey), and he appeared onstage dressed in rags as a beggar. This device of clothing tragic characters in rags was apparently introduced by Euripides, and he is chastised by Aeschylus in Aristophanes' *Frogs* as "the inventor of beggars and stitcher of rags" (lines 842 and 1063–64).

923: Sycophantic sayings. The Greek has "Pandeletean sayings." Pandeletus is found only here and in a fragment of Cratinus' *Cheirons* (fr. 242). The scholia list him as a sycophant and a politician with an odious reputation. He was probably active several years prior to the original production of *Clouds*.

984: Sacrificial beef. This refers to the Buphonia, the sacred sacrifice of a bull to Zeus as part of the Diplolieia festival. Evidently this ancient ceremony had become disdained by the youth of Athens who preferred the dramatic and athletic competitions that were part of other Attic festivals.

990: Manly meat. The Greek has *kôlê* (ham), a euphemism for "penis" (Henderson 1991, pp. 20, 129 n. 100). The Superior Argument regards the young as too weak too lift a warrior's shield and not used to being naked in public due to lack of regular training in the gymnasium.

1012–14: A strapping body. This is a vivid description of the "ideal" male form in Athenian art to the mid-fifth-century B.C.E. This type of male figure can be seen on vase paintings and sculpture of the period, and the male form is discussed at length by Dover (1989, p. 125).

1069: She ran out on him. As with most Greek myths there are different versions of the Peleus and Thetis story. One has Thetis leaving Peleus after he had rebuked her severely (Sophocles fr. 151). Apollodorus of Rhodes (3.13.6) relates how Peleus chastised Thetis for questioning his actions in holding the infant Achilles over a fire to burn off his mortality. Euripides' *Andromache* (1231–83) has the couple reunited, the aged Peleus is given immortality, and they live together in the house of Nereus, Thetis' father, beneath the sea.

1075: Human nature. The conflict between *phusis* ("nature/ spirit") and *nomos* ("custom/laws") was much debated at this time (Plato *Republic* 1. 388 ff., *Gorgias* 482e). It was introduced during the Melian Dialogue (416) as reported by Thucydides (5.105.2) and the "force of nature" argument used to justify political and military conquest.

Stage Direction: Barley. It is not known what was given to Socrates; the scholia write that it was a small sack of barley, although the chorus have mentioned this as an opportunity for making money (line 811), it is clear that Strepsiades is destitute from the evidence of the opening scene (line 29). The offering of such a paltry gift would therefore be an appropriate joke at this point.

1154–66: Then be it known. In the Greek this is a parody of contemporary tragedy. The first two lines are lifted from a play called *Peleus*, by either Sophocles (fr. 491) or Euripides (fr. 623). The final lines are from Euripides' *Hecuba* 171–74.

1195: The new day. Pheidippides uses his new education to twist the meaning of the old-and-new day. He explains that the old day was set aside for settlements, while the new day was when the debts where actually due and could not be demanded until then. He therefore disputes the validity of a system that has confused this and only marks one day for the collection of debts. Strepsiades, suitably befuddled, asks why the courts are allowed to collect on two separate days (the old *and* new day), and Pheidippides replies that they are obviously cheating and this makes any claims against his father through the courts invalid.

1199: Festival taste-testers. According to Athenaeus (4.171c), these were the priests who presided over the Apaturia. This was a local three-day festival organized by each *phratry* (brotherhood). The dining on the first day may have been an exclusive affair and only open to high officials. The second day was the time of the sacrifices and feasting, and the third day was when the infant boys were registered to eventually become full members of the *phratry*. Fathers were required to donate part of their individual sacrifices to the priests, and this may be the practice that Strepsiades is referring to. The actual date of the festival also seems to have been somewhat flexible as long as it fell some time in the month of Pyanepsion (Parke 1997, pp. 89–93).

1216: In this mess. Most lending in fifth-century Athens was between private citizens and not through banks or institutions. A primary source for the borrowing of funds would be family friends and neighbors (*philia*), who would have felt obligated to lend money if they themselves had it to spare. This was tied with Athenian concepts of reciprocity and gift giving that helped cement bonds and relationships within the community as a whole (Millet, pp. 109–26).

1262–64. Doomed, doomed! These lines and the following two spoken by the Second Creditor (1264–65) are from *Licymnius*, by Xenocles (fr. 2). Xenocles was a tragic playwright and the son of Carcinus (see the note on line 1261). These lines were originally spoken by Heracles' mother, Alcmene, on hearing the news of the death of her brother Licymnius at the hand of Tlempolemus. The word "chariot" was probably substituted for "brother" or "loved one" from the original lines now lost.

1287: Interested. The Greek for "interest" is *tokos,* a word that may have its origins in animal husbandry and farming. Farmers without sufficient land to graze their herd would pay a neighbor for grazing rights to his land by offering him a share in the increase of the herd in the form of the newborn calves. In the Greek, Strepsiades retorts, "And what kind of animal might this interest [*tokos*] be?" Plato's *Republic* (507a) contains a similar pun on the word *tokos* in the context of collecting interest.

1325: Strike your own father? The charge of "father beating" was regarded as a particularly vile crime and a slanderous statement under Athenian law (Lysias 10). A law attributed to Solon protected parents from maltreatment by their sons. Under the terms of the law, designed to protect the elderly, sons were expected to provide food and housing and refrain from using any kind of physical assault.

1358: Those kinds of songs. In Plato's *Protagoras* (347a–e) Socrates describes how the guests at a dinner party refuse to hear a song by

Simonides about King Pittacus. They profess that gatherings accompanied by music and singing are the preserve of men who do not possess the intellects to converse intelligently. Plutarch reports Thales having heard women at the grinding stone singing a repetitive song about Pittacus (*Dinner of the Seven Sages* 14).

1414: Alcestis. In this play Admetus is saved from death by the self-sacrifice of his wife, Alcestis, who offers to die in his place. The distraught Admetus turns on his elderly father, Pheres, and cannot understand why he did not offer to die in her place. The quote used is from Pheres' response to his son. He states that he is a free man, and he reminds his son of his fatherly duties. He then tells his son that he values his life, even though he is old and says, "You relish the light of the sun, do you think your father does not" (*Alcestis* line 691).

1422: The way things should be. These views are reflected in Xenophon's *Memorabilia* (1.2.40–47), where Alcibiades is featured asking Socrates about the nature of law.

1478: Hermes. A representation of Hermes in the form of an angular column with a phallus and head of the god stood at points of transition such as crossroads and thresholds of houses (Boardman *GS1*, fig. 169). There may have been such a "Herm" standing outside the stage right door, in contrast to the basin at the stage left door.

1490: Light up a torch. Torches were a regular feature at the end of Old Comedy, and even though Aristophanes had promised in the parabasis that he would not use them (line 543), here they are. They are also found in *Wasps* (line 1331) and *Ecclesiazusae* (lines 978, 1150) and may have appeared in the celebration scenes in *Peace*, *Birds*, and *Frogs*.

Stage Direction: Climb up. A similar scene is found on a mid-fourth-century Paestan bell-crater where one comic character climbs a ladder to a woman in a window and another holds a flaming torch (Green & Handley 1995, fig. 31).

Stage Direction: Enter another student. Sommerstein (1982, note on line 1497) suggests that this could be Chaerephon. For an opposing view see Dover (1968, note on line 1493). The argument hinges on the distribution of parts and the fact that certain manuscripts attribute some lines to Chaerephon while others do not. Chaerephon does make a fleeting appearance as a witness in *Wasps* (line 1412), and it would be hilarious to see the pasty-faced and lurking Chaerephon flushed out into the open by the smoke. This is possible with Aristophanes' four speaking actors if the students and Socrates do not come out of the house but either pop their heads out of windows or open a part of the door, revealing only a mask. This would let one actor quickly play two characters with a swift mask change. As Chaerephon was often presented in the guise of death (Aristophanes' *Birds* 1564), this would have a double dramatic impact on the end of the play. This staging would also allow two actors to play all the parts of the characters in the Pondertorium, negating the need for an extra to play Xanthias.

Appendix: The First Version of *Clouds*

The text of *Clouds* that we possess is not that staged at the Dionysia of 423, which gained the third prize. In *Wasps* and in the revised parabasis of *Clouds* the comedian expresses his displeasure at this result and praises his original version of *Clouds*. If we could be certain whether five comedies or three had been presented, we could more accurately gauge the force of Aristophanes' reaction. Did his excellent comedy finish last of three, or did it get "only the Bronze Medal" in a field of five? In considering the matter of the revision of *Clouds*, the student will want to keep a number of questions in mind. When did Aristophanes make the revision? How extensive were the changes? What in our text belongs to the revised version, and what to the original? How close to production is our text? What are the larger implications for the comedy?

The evidence for the revision comes from a number of sources: Aristophanes' own comments in *Wasps* and in the revised parabasis of *Clouds* (518–62), several references in the scholia to *Clouds* (at 520, 543a, 549a, 553, 591a, 1115a) and at *Wasps* 1038c, one of the hypotheses to *Clouds* (Hypothesis I [Dover]), and finally some fragments assigned by ancient sources to *Clouds*, but which do not appear in the text as we have received it.

Aristophanes tells us about the first *Clouds* twice, first at *Wasps* 1045–50 and later in the parabasis (518–62) of the text of *Clouds* as we have it, where it is clear that we are dealing with a revision—as Dover (*Cl.* lxxx) puts it, a comedy cannot refer to its own failure in the past. However, we should be careful of taking the comedian at face value; of course he will tell us that this was a brilliant comedy that failed to find an appreciative audience and lost to inferior competition. At *Wasps* 1045–50 he describes the play (not named):

> Last year he tried to sow a crop of new ideas,
> BUT YOU JUST DIDN'T GET THE MESSAGE, DID YOU?
> He himself will swear by Dionysus and pour countless libations that no one had ever seen a better comedy. You should feel shame! Shame on you! Let's face it, people, no intelligent person will think badly of our author for being so far ahead of his field that his new concept crashed!

Some believe that the previous lines (1037–42) refer also to first *Clouds*, but "last year" could also signify a comedy at the Lenaea of 423 which was well received and then followed by the "failure" of *Clouds*. I think it safer to identify two productions of 423 here.[1] This theme of novelty and excellence forms the core of Aristophanes' *apologia* at *Clouds* 518–62: "most intellectual of all my comedies" (522), "thwarted by all those hacks" (524), "brand new cutting-edge comedy / every play has something different, something innovative, vivacious, skillful" (547). But he really tells us nothing about the content of the first play or what he is doing differently in the revision.[2]

The scholia do not add a great deal. Σ *Cl.* 552 shows that the ancient scholars knew of only one production date for a *Clouds* by Aristophanes (that in 423); thus the revision was never performed at a festival. Σ *Cl.* 520 tells us that the parabasis was not in the same meter as the original, and Σ *Cl.* 543a that the burning down of the Pondertorium was not in the first version, but this is all that we can glean. The hypothesis, however, gives the most information. The text is difficult and disputed in places; the following is Sommerstein's translation (*Clouds* 4):

> The play is the same as the first, but it has been revised in details, as though the poet intended to produce it again but, for whatever reason,

---

[1] These lines run, "Last year he attacked the demons, plagues, fevers, / and nightmares that came by night to throttle your fathers and choke your grandfathers, / with their subpoenas and writs, their affidavits, and summonses." Then he proceeds, "and what did you do in return? You shunned him!" This suggests that the "plagues, demons," etc., belong to a comedy *before* first *Clouds*.

[2] See Hubbard (1986) for an interesting interpretation of *Cl.* 538 ff. in this regard.

did not do so. To speak generally, there has been revision in every part of the play; some parts have been removed, new sections have been woven in, and changes have been made in arrangement and in the exchanges between characters. Certain parts in their present form belong entirely to the revised version: thus the parabasis of the chorus has been replaced, and where the just argument talks to the unjust, and lastly where the school of Socrates is burned.

It might seem that the revision was extensive; however, there is much that clearly belongs to the 423 version and which would have been altered or replaced, e.g., the rest of the parabasis (especially 575–94), many personal jokes and contemporary references, like that to the war at line 6. One may agree with Sommerstein (*Clouds* 4) that "the revision does not seem to have been as far-reaching as has sometimes been supposed."

That the parabasis proper (518–62) is new is clear from the text itself; it was Aristophanes' response to the results of the competition of 423. It also allows us to date the revision. At 551-58 we hear that Eupolis was the first to attack Hyperbolus in his *Maricas* (421L) and that thereafter Hermippus and everyone else joined in. At the earliest Hermippus and "everyone else" would have produced their plays in 420, and thus the earliest date for Aristophanes' comments would be 419. He mentions Hyperbolus in the present tense (552, 558), and as Hyperbolus was ostracized in 416, we can assume a lower date of 417/16. Thus the revision of *Clouds* belongs to the years 419–417.

The second section singled out as revised is "where the just argument talks to the unjust." But does this mean the verbal scuffle at 899–948, the speech of Superior Argument at 959–1023, or the agon as a whole? The lack of a choral interlude at 888–889 suggests that the reworking began at that point, and that we have only a remnant of a second parabasis at 1115–30 indicates that material was deleted at the end. It seems likely that the agon as a whole was meant, and the changes may have been considerable. A scholion to *Cl.* 889 says that the Arguments were brought on stage in wicker cages, dressed as fighting cocks. There is nothing in our text to suggest such a presentation, and quite probably this comes from the original play.[3] Thus there was an agon between the Arguments in

---

[3] Taplin 101–4 suggests that the "Getty Birds" on a late fifth-century vase are in fact the Arguments of the original *Clouds*.

the original version; changes were made, but we cannot determine how sweeping or extensive these were. I cannot agree with MacDowell when he argues that there was no agon in the original.[4]

Finally, there is the altered ending, which may make all the difference. *Clouds* is unusual in that the "great idea" is reversed and indeed repented of at the end. My own feeling is that there was no such retribution in the first play, that Strepsiades was allowed to get away with not paying his debts, and that the audience (or the judges) did not react well to such an antinomian ending. There is in *Clouds* a subtle tension between sympathy for the not-too-bright farmer and appreciation of intellectual ideas; this may not have gone over well with the audience. Aristophanes may have intended an ironic ending for first *Clouds*, but usually the later scenes are indulgent wish-fulfillments, and that is how I expect that the orginal ended. Thus the revision will have included the chorus's change of attitude, the almost Aeschylean admission of *hybris* at 1462–64, and the retribution wrought by Strepsiades upon Socrates.

The actual fragments of first *Clouds* are not many (K–A III.2, fr. 392–401), and only a few are at all significant:

   fr. 392—This is the fellow [Socrates] who composes those smart-talking clever tragedies for Euripides

   fr. 393—They will lie there like a pair of copulating moths

   fr. 394—They [fem.] are gone in anger down the side of Mount Lycabettus[5]

   fr. 395—Nor will I put a garland around a drinking-cup

Aristophanes then began to revise his *Clouds* sometime between 419 and 417. The revisions were extensive in that he made alterations in all parts of the comedy, but only three major changes in the text can be documented: the parabasis proper, the contest between the Arguments (and here we do not know how much was altered), and the end of the comedy with its retribution against

---

[5] "They" are certainly the chorus of Clouds; at line 323 of our text they are seen approaching from Mount Parnes.

Socrates. The comedy was nowhere near production when he abandoned the project.[6] The topical allusions and personal jokes of the 423 version are still in the text,[7] as is most of the parabasis. Thus it is dangerous to consider what we have as a complete and integrated text and to treat it in the manner that we do other comedies. Two further questions remain and are perhaps unanswerable: (a) how did a partly revised version survive as a text? and (b) how did it displace the version of 423 that was actually produced?

I.C.S.

---

[6] Fisher and Kopff, however, maintain that the revision was almost complete and ready for the theatre.

[7] On this see Storey (1993) 78–81.

Further Reading

The bibliography on Aristophanes is immense. The following is intended to guide one's first reading, and to suggest some more advanced and specialized studies for those interested in going further.

Texts

Four overall editions of the Greek text can be mentioned, plus the scholarly editions of individual plays. The Oxford Classical Text of Hall and Geldart, *Aristophanis Comoediae*, 2 vols. (Oxford 1906) is very outdated; a newer version is being prepared by N. G. Wilson. The Budé version of V. Coulon (Paris 1923–) is better, but also in need of replacement. A. H. Sommerstein has completed the Aris and Philips series (in 12 volumes) of The Comedies of Aristophanes, with introduction, text with literal translation, and commentary (Warminster 1980–2003). Finally J. Henderson has re-edited Aristophanes in four volumes for the Loeb Classical Library (Cambridge, MA 1998–2002).

For the individual comedies the following may be recommended (in addition to Sommerstein):

Acharnians	—by S. D. Olson (Oxford 2002)
Knights	—in preparation for the Oxford/Clarendon series (J. Henderson)
Clouds	—by K. J. Dover (Oxford 1968)
Wasps	—by D. M. MacDowell (Oxford 1971)
Peace	—by S. D. Olson (Oxford 1998)
Birds	—by N. V. Dunbar (Oxford 1995)

Lysistrata	—by J. Henderson (Oxford 1987)
Thesmophoriazusae	—by C. Austin and S. D. Olson (Oxford 2004)
Frogs	—by W. G. Stanford (London 1963)
	by K. J. Dover (Oxford 1993)
Ecclesiazusae	—by R. G. Ussher (Oxford 1973)

For the fragments of the lost plays of Aristophanes and the other poets of Old Comedy, the student is now referred to R. Kassel and C. Austin, *Poetae Comici Graeci*, vol. II, III.2 (Aristophanes), IV–VIII (Berlin/New York 1983–).

General Studies

P. Cartledge, *Aristophanes and His Theatre of the Absurd* (London 1990)

K. J. Dover, *Aristophanic Comedy* (London 1972)

E. Handley, "Comedy," in *Cambridge History of Classical Literature*, vol. 1, *Greek Literature*, B. M. W. Knox and P. Easterling, eds. (Cambridge 1985) 103–46

D. M. MacDowell, *Aristophanes and Athens* (Oxford 1995)

K. McLeish, *The Theatre of Aristophanes* (London 1980)

G. Murray, *Aristophanes* (Oxford 1933)

G. Norwood, *Greek Comedy* (London 1931)

F. H. Sandbach, *The Comic Theatre of Greece and Rome* (London 1985) ch. 1–3

R. G. Ussher, *Aristophanes* (Oxford 1979)

Specialized Studies

A. M. Bowie, *Aristophanes: Myth, Ritual, and Comedy* (Cambridge 1993)

C. W. Dearden, *The Stage of Aristophanes* (London 1976)

V. Ehrenberg, *The People of Aristophanes*, 2nd ed. (Oxford 1951)

T. Gelzer, *Die epirrhematische Agon bei Aristophanes* (Munich 1960)

J. Henderson, *The Maculate Muse*, 2nd ed. (Oxford 1991)

T. Hubbard, *The Mask of Comedy: Aristophanes and the Intertextual Parabasis* (Austin 1991)

L. P. E. Parker, *The Songs of Aristophanes* (Oxford 1997)

K. J. Reckford, *Aristophanes' Old and New Comedy* (Chapel Hill 1987)

G. M. Sifakis, *Parabasis and Animal Choruses* (London 1971)

M. Silk, *Aristophanes and the Definition of Comedy* (Oxford 2000)

N. W. Slater, *Spectator Politics: Metatheatre and Performance in Aristophanes* (Philadelphia 2002)

C. H. Whitman, *Aristophanes and the Comic Hero* (Cambridge MA 1964)

B. Zimmermann, *Untersuchungen zur Form und dramatischen Technik der Aristophanischen Komödien* (Königstein 1984–87)

Collections of Essays

G. Dobrov, ed., *The City as Comedy* (Chapel Hill/London 1997)

D. Harvey and J. Wilkins, eds., *The Rivals of Aristophanes* (London 2000)

J. Henderson, ed., *Aristophanes: essays in interpretation*, *YCS* 26 (1980)

E. Segal, ed., *Oxford Readings in Aristophanes* (Oxford 1996)

A. H. Sommerstein et al., eds., *Tragedy, Comedy and the Polis* (Bari 1993)

J. Winkler and F. Zeitlin, ed., *Nothing to Do with Dionysus?* (Princeton 1990)

Visual Evidence

J. Barron, *An Introduction to Greek Sculpture* (London 1965)

J. Boardman, *Greek Sculpture—The Archaic Period* (London 1978) [*GS1*]

————, *Greek Sculpture—The Classical Period* (London 1978) [*GS2*]

————, *Athenian Black Figure Vases* (London 1974) [*ABFV*]

————, *Athenian Red Figure Vases—The Archaic Period* (London 1974) [*ARFV1*]

————, *Athenian Red Figure Vases—The Classical Period* (London 1989) [*ARFV2*]

I. Brooke, *Costume in Greek Classic Drama* (London 1973)

J. McK. Camp II, *The Athenian Agora: A Guide to the Excavation and Museum* (Athenian School of Classical Studies 1990)

R. Green and E. Handley, *Images of the Greek Theatre* (London 1995)

R. A. Higgins, *Greek Terracottas* (London 1967)

B. Sparkes, "The Greek Kitchen," *Journal of Hellenic Studies* 82 (1962) 121–37

————, "Illustrating Aristophanes," *Journal of Hellenic Studies* 95 (1975) 122–35

B. Sparkes and L. Talbot, *Pots and Pans of Classical Athens* (American School of Classical Studies at Athens 1959)

O. Taplin, *Comic Angels* (Oxford 1993)

A. D. Trendall and T. B. L. Webster, *Illustrations of Greek Drama* (London 1971)

Related Studies

W. Burkert, *Greek Religion* [tr. J. Raffian] (Oxford 1985)

———, *Homo Necans* [tr. P. Bing] (Berkeley/London 1983)

K. J. Dover, *Greek Homosexuality*, 2nd ed. (Cambridge MA 1989)

D. M. MacDowell, *The Law in Classical Athens* (London 1978)

R. Meiggs and D. M. Lewis, eds., *A Selection of Greek Historical Inscriptions*, 2nd ed. (Oxford 1988)

J. Mikalson, *Athenian Popular Religion* (Chapel Hill/London 1983)

P. Millett, *Lending and Borrowing in Ancient Athens* (Cambridge 1992)

H. W. Parke, *Festivals of the Athenian* (London 1977)

R. Parker, *Miasma, Pollution and Purification in Early Greek Religion* (Oxford 1983)

Significant Articles

A. M. Bowie, "Thinking with Drinking: Wine and the Symposium in Aristophanes," *Journal of Hellenic Studies* 117 (1997) 1–21

C. Carey, "Comic Ridicule and Democracy," in *Ritual, Finance and Politics*, R. Osborne and S. Hornblower, eds. (Oxford 1994) 69–83

G. E. M. de Ste Croix, "The Political Outlook of Aristophanes," Appendix XXIX in *The Origins of the Peloponnesian War* (Ithaca 1972) 355–76

J. Gardner, "Aristophanes and Male Anxiety—The defence of the *oikos*," *Greece & Rome* 36 (1989) 51–62

A. W. Gomme, "Aristophanes and Politics," *Classical Review* 52 (1938) 97–109

S. Halliwell, "Aristophanic Satire," *Yearbook of English Studies* 14 (1984) 6–20

M. Heath, "Aristophanes and His Rivals," *Greece & Rome* 37 (1990) 143–58

M. Silk, "The People of Aristophanes," in *Characterization and Individuality in Greek Literature*, C. Pelling, ed. (Oxford 1990) 150–73

A. H. Sommerstein, "How to Avoid Being a *Komodoumenos*," *Classical Quarterly* 46 (1996) 327–56

I. C. Storey, "Cutting Comedies," in J. Barsby, ed., *Greek and Roman Drama: Translation and Performance*, Drama 12 (Stuttgart 2002) 146–67

———, "Poets, Politicians, and Perverts," *Classics Ireland* 5 (1998) 85–134

R. Wycherley, "Aristophanes and Euripides," *Greece & Rome* 15 (1946) 98–107

Bibliographies

For further reading on Aristophanes and Old Comedy the student is directed to the yearly surveys in *L'Année Philologique* (*APh*). Most recent studies are well supplied with bibliographies. I would call attention to the extensive bibliography in Sommerstein et al. (1993), the introduction to Segal's *Oxford Readings*, and my own two survey articles, "Old Comedy 1975–1984" in *Echos du Monde Classique* 31 (1987) 1–46, and "Δέκατον μὲν ἔτος τόδ': Old Comedy 1982-1991," *Antichthon* 26 (1992) 1–29.

One final work must be mentioned: E. Csapo and W. J. Slater, *The Context of Ancient Drama* (Ann Arbor 1994), which presents the ancient sources for drama (in translation), a fair and informed commentary, a brief bibliography by topic, and some very useful illustrations.

Suggested Readings for Clouds

Commentaries

K. J. Dover, *Aristophanes Clouds* (Oxford 1968)

A. H. Sommerstein, *The Comedies of Aristophanes*, vol. III *Clouds* (Warminster 1982)

Books

R. K. Fisher, *Aristophanes Clouds: Purpose and Technique* (Amsterdam 1984)

M. C. Marianetti, *Religion and Politics in Aristophanes' Clouds* (Hildesheim 1992)

D. O'Regan, *Rhetoric, Comedy, and the Violence of Language in Aristophanes' Clouds* (New York/Oxford 1992)

Book Chapters

The chapters in the following may be consulted with profit; full details are found in the general list of further readings: Bowie (1993) 102–33, Cartledge 22–31, Dover (1972) 101–20, Hubbard 88–112, MacDowell (1995) 113–49, Murray 85–105, Norwood 211–32, Reckford 388–402, Whitman 119–43.

Articles

L. Edmunds, "Aristophanes' Socrates," in *Proceedings of the Boston area colloquium in ancient philosophy* 1 (1986): 209–30

P. Green, "Strepsiades, Socrates, and the Abuses of Intellectualism," *Greek, Roman and Byzantine Studies* 20 (1979): 1–17

J. Henderson, "Problems in Greek Literary History: the case of *Clouds*," in *Nomodeiktes*, R. M. Rosen and J. Farrell, eds. (Ann Arbor 1993): 591–601

T. K. Hubbard, "Parabatic Self-Criticism and the Two Versions of Aristophanes' *Clouds*," *Classical Antiquity* 5 (1986): 182–97

K. Kleve, "Anti-Dover or Socrates in the *Clouds,*" *Symbolae Osloneses* 48 (1983): 23–37

E. C. Kopff, "The Date of Aristophanes, *Nubes* II," *American Journal of Philology* 111 (1990): 318–29

T. Long, "Understanding Comic Action in Aristophanes," *Classical World* 70 (1976): 1–8

M. Nussbaum, "Aristophanes and Socrates on Learning Practical Wisdom," *Yale Classical Studies* 26 (1980): 43–97

K. J. Reckford, "Strepsiades as a Comic Ixion," *Illinois Classical Studies* 16 (1991): 125–36

C. Segal, "Aristophanes' Cloud-Chorus," *Arethusa* 2 (1967): 143–61

I. C. Storey, "The Dates of Aristophanes' *Clouds* II and Eupolis' *Baptai,*" *American Journal of Philology* 114 (1993): 71–84

H. Tarrant, "Midwifery in the *Clouds,*" *Classical Quarterly* 38 (1988): 116–22

———, "Alcibiades in Aristophanes' *Clouds* I and II," *Ancient History: Resources for Teachers* 19 (1989): 13–20

———, "*Clouds* I; Steps toward Reconstruction," *Arctos* 25 (1991): 157–81

L. Woodbury, "Strepsiades' Understanding," *Phoenix* 34 (1980): 108–27

The following studies barely scratch the surface of the matter of the first version of *Clouds*: Dover (*Cl.*) lxxx–xcviii, Fisher 20–23, Henderson (1993), Hubbard (1986), Kopff, MacDowell (1995) 134–49, O'Regan 133–39, Sommerstein (*Cl.*) 3f., Storey (1993), and Tarrant (1989) and (1991). Fuller citations appear in the list above.